Dear Readers...

For many years our "From The Manse Window"
feature has inspired and brought comfort to the
readers of "The People's Friend". Due to its popularity,
we now bring you this souvenir book containing a
collection of these much-loved messages for you
to enjoy throughout the church year.

Contents

Where It All *Began*

Discover the origins of "From The Manse Window".

FROM around the 1900s, a religious message was included in "The People's Friend".

This new article came about following a discussion in the correspondents' pages of the "Friend". The debate was centred on whether the magazine, being fiction-based, could in all conscience be regarded as appropriate for Sunday reading.

The letters flew back and forth, some from ministers' wives and even the clergy themselves, all assuring readers that the wholesome nature and upright values of the "Friend" lent themselves wholeheartedly to Sunday reading.

Indeed, one minister claimed to quote from it in his sermons, while again and again readers claimed to take inspiration from its pages.

But it was following this debate that the magazine introduced a regular article entitled "For Sunday Afternoon", which ran for the next few years.

It contained a Bible verse for reading, then background information and a brief discourse on that week's theme, ending with a short prayer.

The article first appeared in 1910 and was written by one Fergus Mackenzie, the pen name of the Rev. James Anderson of Dyce, Aberdeenshire.

It would seem, therefore, that "Fergus Mackenzie" was the "Friend's" first minister-contributor.

Decades passed, and then, in 1958, a new voice was heard. The beloved reverend of St Andrew's church in Dundee, T.R.S. (Tom) Campbell, wrote for the "Friend" for twenty-seven years in total.

His warm style and wise thoughts are as fresh today as they were back then.

Take his first New Year greeting:

"May you stand in the dawn-light of 1959 with new strength for old burdens. And may you write happiness across the yet-unwritten page of the coming year."

One current member of staff blesses his advice every time she tackles the steep walk to the top of the Hilltown in the city.

"I have a few parishioners in this part of the town. When I walk up, I have learned to keep my eyes on the pavement below my feet, focusing on my next step, rather than the rise before me."

His passing was a great loss to all at the "Friend", as can be seen in this eulogy, written by the editor of the time, in 1985.

"'Friend' readers, I know, will miss him greatly and will wish to treasure his memory.

"That is why, over the weeks ahead, we are proposing to reprint a selection of those articles which were most highly regarded by readers.

"It is a way of paying tribute to a remarkable and well-loved man, and helping to keep that memory alive."

For the next several months that was what we did.

It would be some years before a new batch of ministers introduced themselves. Now offering words of wisdom and comfort in "From The Manse Window", these contributors quickly became "Friend" favourites.

The following names will certainly be familiar to readers: the Rev. Dr James Martin, the Rev. David Bryant, the Rev. Ian Petrie and the Rev. Ian W.F. Hamilton.

Today a wide range of writers appear on the page now called "On Reflection".

Sister Tessa Fisk is a nun based at Lindisfarne, Holy Island, while Kathrine Davey is a lay Methodist preacher.

Whatever paths have led these talented people here, we are delighted, as we always have been, to pass on their words of wisdom and encouragement to our readers, so many of whom take deep comfort and support from their writings. ■

"May you stand in the dawn-light with new strength for old burdens."
January 1959

Tom Campbell with his dog, Rebel.

D.C. Thomson.

9

If someone asks, "How are you?" you might reply "Not bad" or "OK, I suppose". These answers indicate that your mind is in a downbeat mood. By answering in another way, like "Fantastic, thanks!" or "Wonderful!" your mind will focus on the upbeat, and you'll feel more energised. Try it and let it become a habit.

The
Church
Year

**The Church Year is an annual cycle
which allows us to remember
Jesus's life, death and resurrection
and to celebrate the
gift of the Holy Spirit.**

The Coming Of
Christb

By Rev. Barbara Mosse

DOESN'T everything seem to happen in a rush these days? Technology has improved our quality of life in many ways, but it's not all good news.

Computers were originally meant to speed up our rate of work so that there would be more time for leisure, but all that seems to have happened is that they've made time available for yet more work!

Although it's lovely to be able to order a book online with the click of a button, is it really necessary for me to pay extra for a service which will deliver it to me the very next day? Whatever happened to the lost art of waiting, and the joys of anticipation?

The season of Advent begins a new round of the Church's year. Advent means "coming", and during this period we celebrate the coming of our Lord Jesus Christ as a baby in Bethlehem.

This time is likely to be busy, with cakes and puddings to make, trees to decorate and cards to post.

We will order gifts online, or steel ourselves to brave the pre-Christmas mayhem of shopping centres, and breathe a sigh of relief when everything has been ticked off the list.

But Advent also offers us a priceless gift which cuts across the grain of this excitement – an invitation to take time out from the rush of Christmas preparations to be quiet.

To sit in our Father's presence,

iStock.

for just a few moments each day, to wait and prepare our hearts for the coming of the Christ Child.

We may not realise that there are three advents to celebrate, not just one. The first looks back to Old Testament times, long before the birth of Jesus.

The Israelites' long "night" of waiting for his coming lasted many generations, with the people seeing themselves like watchmen on the city walls, straining their eyes for the first hint of the coming dawn.

They looked forward to the coming of the Messiah, the one who would release them from captivity and oppression. The haunting Advent hymn "O Come, O Come, Emmanuel" captures this spirit of ancient waiting and longing beautifully.

But it's not all about looking back. The second advent encourages us to look forward, to the promised second coming of Jesus at the end of time.

Christ spoke about this, and the Advent hymn "Lo, He Comes With Clouds Descending" expresses this aspect of our faith poetically and beautifully.

How long it will be before Christ returns we don't know. But the invitation is still the same: to wait patiently in faith and hope, trusting in the love and goodness of our Lord.

We may fear we'll get a bit lost between the remote past and the distant future, but the third aspect of Advent points to the Christ who stands with us now, right where we are.

Christ offers us a personal invitation – to welcome his coming to us individually, and to trust him with all our joy and pain, our hopes and fears:

"Come, thou long-expected Jesus, born to set thy people free;

From our fears and sins release us; let us find our rest in thee."

Happy Advent. ∎

Life's
Journey

By Kathrine Davey, Mansfield Methodist preacher

ADVENT is the time of year when we start journeying towards our celebrations of the birth of Christ, and that set me thinking about the journeys that we all take and the journeys mentioned in the Bible in the run-up to Christmas.

I was sitting on the bus, travelling to speak in a church that I didn't know. A bus journey can be quite sociable – depending on our fellow travellers, of course. It is often very rare for us to be alone on a bus.

While thinking of journeys, I was reminded of that great Christian story "Pilgrim's Progress". The hero, Christian, depends on the others who travel with him to help him cope with the obstacles that confront him. When the Eternal City, his goal, is in sight, Christian and his friend Hopeful must cross a river without a bridge. Christian nearly drowns, but Hopeful reminds him of Christ's love, and Christian emerges safely from the water.

When we make preparations for a journey, there are certain objects that are often necessary. The first to come to mind is an umbrella. Although these are not mentioned in the Bible, there is an appropriate verse in the Psalms that says:

"But let all who take refuge in you be glad, Let them ever sing for joy. Spread your protection over them, that those who love your name may rejoice in you."

I think God's protection and guidance is far more useful than any other way of sheltering.

Another necessity for a journey might be to have a pair of

iStock.

sunglasses to hand. Again the Psalmist has an appropriate quotation when he assures of God's protection with these words: "The sun will not harm you by day, nor the moon by night."

I am sure we can think of other things that we might use – a good stout pair of walking boots might be essential for some outings, or a pair of binoculars might be useful if we get a chance to glimpse the wonders of God's creation.

My own journey was quite short, yet the Christmas journey that probably sticks in the mind most was probably the longest:

"Wise men seeking Jesus
Travelled from afar."

We cannot be sure where they came from – all we are told is they came "from the east", but it was certain that it took a long time.

They must have used their fellow travelling companions to provide encouraging conversation. The gospels tell us they became "overjoyed" when the star showed where Jesus was.

Another Christmas journey is that of Mary and Joseph, journeying from Nazareth to Bethlehem. This journey could not have been more different – the young couple must have had a difficult time travelling, although I like to imagine that they were both comforting and encouraging each other on. They must have seen plenty of other travellers on the route, and known they faced a difficult time ahead.

I haven't space to mention the many other journeys in the Bible, although some may come to mind as you journey through life. Just be careful who you travel with! ■

Christ, Our
Saviour

By Rev. Ian W.F. Hamilton

MANY "Friend" readers may have seen a mini-drama series on TV about the career of Cilla Black, and many of you, like me, will be able to remember Cilla's scintillating song of the swinging Sixties – the theme song from the film of the same name, "Alfie". The question posed in the opening line of that hit song was, "What's it all about, Alfie?"

I would like to transpose that question from the film scene to the manger scene!

"What's it all about?"

We must ask that question because there are still many who, while they gladly celebrate it, don't know what this massive, festive, votive, superlative celebration that the world calls Christmas is about!

The season is one of festival and festivity the world over, extending even to non-Christian lands. With it comes the traditional adornment of streets, houses and churches; the pageantry of lights and song; the giving of gifts and the sentiments of goodwill and peace. We eat, drink and make merry. We rejoice!

However, as we do these things, we often lose sight of what Christmas is really all about. Let us pause for a moment from the mad seasonal scramble and address the question to ourselves once again.

"What's it all about?"

Quite simply, it's about a baby. A baby born over 2,000 years ago whose mother's name was Mary and whose father's name was Joseph. The baby was given the name Jesus which means "Saviour". The stories surrounding his birth are vividly brought to mind in the symbols of the season which, at this time of year, are all around us – stars, shepherds, kings,

iStock.

camels, sheep, cattle and a manger.

Yet Christmas isn't all about symbolism and stories, though these help to set the scene for the annual celebration. First and foremost, Christmas is about a baby named Jesus.

Why do we still get so excited and worked up about a baby born so long ago? We don't make any similar fuss about Socrates or Alexander the Great or any of the mighty Caesars. So we must ask why, year after year, should this baby stir up such festivity throughout the world?

Let me make some suggestions. This special baby grew up to be a wise and good man. We don't know much about his childhood; in his youthful years he became a carpenter. Some of the words he spoke are known to this day, and they still ring with truth.

Many stories of what he did have been faithfully recorded and carefully preserved, and reveal his care, concern and love for all his fellow men and women.

But there must be something more to Christmas than remembering a wise and good man. And, of course, there is. This good man became the saviour of men and women.

"To you is born this day in the City of David a Saviour, Christ the Lord!" was the angel's message to the shepherds. And throughout his short life this baby Saviour lived up to his name by forgiving people their shortcomings and their sins. He saved them by dying on a cross, and many believe that his death, in a unique way, had God's almighty and immortal power within it to save all mankind.

This is why we celebrate Christmas. Because that baby became a saviour – the baby in the manger, the saviour on the cross . . . that's the full story. In answer to the question posed by Cilla's song, that's what it's all about.

If you are in two minds as to whether it will make a difference to your life to keep that baby at the centre of it during this time of festivity and celebration, try it and see!

A very happy and blessed Christmas to you all. ■

Bless This

House

By Janice Ross

A FEW years ago, while on holiday in the south of Germany, I was intrigued to see that many of the houses had chalk symbols above their front doors.

At the time of my visit this is the one I saw: 20 + C + M + B + 08.

I discovered that this is a tradition called Chalking The Door, which is carried out by many Christians at the time of Epiphany or Twelfth Night.

This usually takes place on January 6, which is the day when we remember the visiting of the Christ Child by the Three Wise Men.

The chalked numbers denote the year. This year they will say, 20 + C + M + B + 18.

The letters have two meanings. Firstly they are the initials of the traditional names of the Three Magi: Caspar, Melchior and Balthazar.

They are also the abbreviations for the Latin words *Christus mansionem benedicat* meaning "May Christ bless this house".

This Epiphany House Blessing is an invitation for Jesus to be a daily guest to the home in the coming year.

The homeowners are welcoming Jesus into their home and asking that he watch over and bless all those who live in this house and all who visit.

It shows an awareness of the need for God's provision and protection and also a gratitude for his involvement in the life of the family.

This reminder is similar to another tradition which many will

remember from childhood.

On visiting the homes of many fisherfolk in the north-east of Scotland it was very common to see a framed picture above the dining table, called the Unseen Guest.

These words were often cross stitched.

"Christ is the Head of this home,

The Unseen Guest at every meal, The Silent Listener to every conversation."

For the adults this would have been a reverent reminder of Christ's presence, while for any visiting children it may have struck a warning to be on their best behaviour! Grace would, of course, have also been said before meals.

The idea behind both of these traditions is to heighten our awareness of the Saviour's presence.

Holman Hunt, in his famous painting the Light Of The World, wanted to portray that the Saviour of the world is alive today and will dwell in the hearts of all those who admit him.

In his painting there is a heavy door, with rusty nails and hinges, and overgrown with ivy. There is no handle on the door, suggesting that the door is opened from the inside. Jesus is standing at the door, a lantern in his hand, and is knocking.

"May I come in?" would be the interpretation.

Jesus not only wants to dwell in our homes, at our meal tables, but in our very hearts. He wants to make his home in our hearts and to abide with us for ever. ■

Spread A Little
Happiness

By Rev. David Bryant

TAKING assembly was never a popular task at the large London comprehensive school at which I used to teach.

Addressing several hundred children was often rather challenging, particularly if it was a Monday morning and the pupils were unenthusiastic at the thought of beginning another week of school.

The biggest hurdle was thinking of something that would not only grip their attention, but give a worthwhile message.

One of the school's year heads was especially good at this job, though, and I remember clearly a talk that she used to give each year to the new intake.

It was based on an old fable and gave the children something to think about.

The story concerned a man who was travelling on foot from Thessalonika to Athens. He saw a party of men and women coming towards him and decided to sound them out as to what sort of a welcome he would receive in the city.

One of the men frowned and shook his head.

"The people of Athens are a mean lot. They overcharge for rooms, give you short change in the shops and cannot even be bothered to greet you with a 'good morning'."

A woman continued the tale at this point.

"I have never come across such

a bad-tempered, miserable-faced bunch of citizens. If I were you I would turn round and go back the way you came."

By this time the traveller was beginning to feel rather worried, for he had journeyed a very long distance, was tired and footsore and also feeling very hot because it was high summer.

The final straw came when another man chipped in.

"Watch your pockets," he warned him. "If you are not careful your money will be stolen and your bag snatched."

The group went on their way, leaving the words ringing in the man's ears.

He was on the point of turning back when another group came along the road leading from the town.

"How did you find Athens, friends?"

Back came many cheerful replies.

"I've never come across such generous, helpful people as the Athenians."

Another one spoke.

"Goodness is stronger than evil"

"They are as honest as the day is long and very generous, sometimes slipping an extra cake in your bag at the bakery."

A woman added her own comment.

"I lost my way and the passers-by were so kind," she told him with a smile. "One of them came out with a drink of water to cool me down."

"You won't find a more welcoming, happy town in the whole of Greece," another traveller added.

The moral of this story is clear. Some people will always moan and complain and speak badly of others, constantly spreading misery and gloom, while others like to see the good in people, to notice small kindnesses, return smiles and respond to friendly remarks.

Here is a prayer of encouragement that helps us view God's world cheerfully.

Goodness is stronger than evil.
Love is stronger than hate.
Light is stronger than darkness.
Thankfulness is stronger than ingratitude. ∎

Working
Together

By Kathrine Davey, Mansfield Methodist preacher

THE other day at church I helped the children (and many others) to make a fruit salad. It wasn't a real one, but a combination of various coloured pieces of paper.

I began with grapes. We all took a "grape" to represent the idea that we all had something valuable to put into the fruit bowl and make a difference. After all, one grape isn't much by itself, but if we all pool our gifts then it becomes a tasty bunch.

When I asked who of the group liked grapes, several people shook their heads. So I produced pictures of different fruit and told everyone they could pick the one that they preferred.

Many coloured in their pictures, often very imaginatively, but some of the older members of the church were reluctant to join in this spirit of creativity.

When I explained that these were to represent the gifts we had to offer to the church, and to God, some of the older people there wrote a note on their paper outlining the gifts that they had to offer.

Then I went round with a bowl, and gathered the many pieces of the "fruit" together, to make the point that, although gifts are good when they come singly, putting them all together and mixing them up makes a healthy, balanced diet both for us and in our church life.

The fruit bowls were brought up to the front of the church with the financial offerings, and so our

iStock.

lives and our money were dedicated together.

My point was also illustrated by someone sitting on a table, blocking the view of the computer screen at the front of the church, where the words of the songs were displayed.

She did as she had been told and refused to move, and so we had no choice but to move the table. However, one person could not do this single-handedly, and thus had to call to another church friend to help.

Even the two of them were unable to lift the table and so a third person was called.

Only when a fourth pair of hands was added were the helpers able to lift the table, together with its occupant, and move it out of the way, to the cheers of everyone in the congregation.

In order to succeed, the people concerned had to be prepared to work together. This event put me in mind of the time when Jesus healed a paralysed man who had been let down through the roof by his friends so that he could reach Jesus, who was surrounded by crowds.

I'm sure he was glad that he was let down by a number of friends, so that the mat he was on was supported properly.

After all, if just one or two of his friends had taken it into their heads to move him, who knows how he would have maintained his balance, and he would probably have rolled into one corner of the mat.

So that is probably why one gospel specifically points out that there were four friends.

Jesus commended their behaviour and rewarded them by healing their friend: a result that could have ended in disaster if they hadn't been prepared to act together.

In other words, the church needs us all to help one another in order to achieve our goals. ■

Trust In
Him

By Rev. Susan Sarapuk

PLAY the guitar and lead worship during communion at the midweek service in our parish church. I had a conversion experience when I was a student in London and one of the first things I did was to learn to play the guitar so that I could worship.

Unfortunately, lately I've developed arthritis in one of my fingers and the swollen joint is reaching the point where soon I won't be able to hold down the strings on the fretboard. It's already very painful when I play.

That's frustrating, particularly as I know that playing the guitar is an important part of my worship and helps others to worship, too.

There are other stresses and frustrations in my life at the moment. No doubt in yours, too. Rung the local surgery on a

Monday to try to get a doctor's appointment lately, anyone?

Often we question what our faith really means. Surely, if we're Christians, we should be able to trust in God in all circumstances, and not get frustrated over things? We should be serene and at peace.

I remember what Paul wrote about sin in his letter to the Romans – the fact that we know what is right, that we want to do the right thing, yet instead we do the very thing we know we shouldn't. There's a man who was speaking from experience.

And that, he says, is sin living in us. It's no excuse, but it does help us to understand that we are living in a fallen world, that we're not perfect and we never will be in this life. So we're going to get frustrated and we're going to make mistakes

from time to time.

Learning to trust God, who says, "Your ways are not my ways," is a lifetime's journey. We are being educated to "become mature, attaining to the whole measure of the fullness of Christ." That doesn't happen overnight and often it's the tough times that promote growth in our faith.

We're encouraged to consider the whole picture; to know that God is in control of our destiny even though, at times, we become frustrated at things that happen . . . or don't happen. A great example, once again, is Paul, who was called to be an evangelist. He travelled, he preached, he established churches and he went back to visit them.

How frustrating, then, to find himself a prisoner in Rome. Yet, far from getting frustrated, he could see God's purpose in his imprisonment, understanding that even in his confinement he was being used to spread the gospel.

Commander Jim Lovell of the ill-fated Apollo 13 mission warned his crew, when they were getting tetchy with each other and were not sure if they would make it back to earth, that they could spend the next ten minutes bouncing off the walls but they would only end up back where they started – trying to figure out how to stay alive.

Our circumstances change. Getting older means our health changes. We might not be able to do the things we used to do, but God's not done with us. So, if you're frustrated, let off steam, by all means. But then say, "All right, Lord, I know you're in control."

We always come back to where we started – God's love and purpose for us.

No matter your age, no matter your health or mobility problems, there is always one thing we can do. Pray. And I've noticed that when I focus on others through prayer, instead of focusing on myself, my frustration goes away. ■

Scientists believe there is no such thing as luck. People expect good or bad things to happen to them and that reflects in their expectations of life. If you expect good things, you're the optimist, the "lucky" one. So be lucky: start expecting the good things today!

Fishers Of
Men

By Rev. David Bryant

PERHAPS you have noticed a car with a sticker of a fish in the back window at some time and have wondered what it meant. Maybe you have seen somebody wearing a badge shaped like a fish and been curious.

The fish, in fact, is a very ancient Christian symbol.

The Gospels of the Bible are full of stories that make mention of fish.

Some of the first disciples had been out all night fishing but had caught nothing. When they returned to land Jesus told them to cast their net on the other side of the boat.

The result was a large catch of fish. Later on he told the disciples that their role in the Christian life was to be fishers of men.

The story of the feeding of the 5,000 is a familiar one to us all.

A great crowd had followed Jesus to a remote area and had forgotten to bring picnics. They were tired and very hungry.

A young boy had a packed lunch consisting of bread and fish.

Jesus told the disciples to distribute the meagre lunch amongst the people and, miraculously, every person there had enough to eat.

In one of the resurrection appearances of Christ, fish again play a part.

When the disciples returned from an overnight fishing trip they noticed a charcoal fire burning on the beach.

Curious to see who had lit a bonfire so early in the morning,

they walked across the sand towards it.

Jesus was there, standing by the fire, cooking fish over the embers. He told the disciples to bring some of their catch to him.

Jesus cooked sufficient fish for them all to eat and they then sat down to a shared breakfast.

Fish are so much a part of the Gospels that it was only natural that the early Christians should use them as a symbol of their faith.

However, there are other reasons why the fish became a secret sign.

Under Roman emperors such as Nero and Diocletian, the Christians were savagely persecuted, and their lives were continually in danger.

In order to escape possible torture and death they met in the catacombs – or underground burial chambers – that lay all around Rome.

Here the followers held their services, and to communicate with each other they thought up a secret sign.

The opening letters of the Greek words for Jesus, Christ, God, Son and Saviour spell out the word *ichthus* which is another Greek word meaning "fish".

It was an ideal symbol for them to use. Anybody could quickly draw the outline of a fish. The fish symbol summed up their faith in Jesus very neatly.

There is a tradition that in the early days of Christianity, if a Christian met a stranger he would draw half the outline of a fish in the dust with the toe of his shoe.

If the other person completed the drawing he knew that he was talking to somebody who was sympathetic towards the faith.

The tradition has continued through the ages and some churchgoers still wear earrings, brooches or necklaces with fish symbols on them as a sign that they follow Christ.

So, if you are sitting in a traffic jam and notice a fish sticker on the car in front, you will know what it means! ∎

God's Plan

By Rev. Susan Sarapuk

LAST week in our Bible group we were studying the conversion of St Paul and how Ananias was instrumental in helping him take that final step into faith.

To me the incredible thing wasn't so much the words – "The Lord Jesus who appeared to you on the road as you were coming here has sent me so that you may see again and be filled with the Holy Spirit" – amazing though they are, but that Ananias first placed his hands on Paul and addressed him as Brother Saul.

This hater of Christians, this destroyer of the church, this enemy of all that Ananias stood for, heard the words "Brother Saul". It can't have been easy for Ananias to say those words; he must have been very afraid, even though God had spoken clearly to him.

"Are you sure, Lord?" he seems to ask. "Did I hear you right? Do you know who this man is?"

That's what we would do, isn't it?

Yet, even though the notion that Saul would become a Christian seemed fantastic, Ananias obeyed. He wasn't an exceptional or special believer. He'd just learned how to trust God.

Often we fail to trust God because we think we know better. We say, "No, God couldn't possibly have meant that!" and we do our own thing.

If only we would trust that he really does have everything under control and that we slot into his plan! Who would have thought that the passionate Jew, so proud of his heritage, would become known for his ministry to the Gentiles?

But God had planned it that way

iStock.

and Ananias became part of that plan.

I wonder how Paul must have felt. He'd had an encounter with the Living Jesus, challenging everything he'd believed in and held dear.

His plan to be riding into Damascus in triumph, proud of his authority to persecute the church, had been scuttled and instead he had been humbled.

Imagine how terrified he must have been at losing his sight; as far as he knew he would be blind for the rest of his life. How would he live like that? He would be for ever dependent on others; everything he held dear, everything he had become, was lost to him.

Then a stranger appeared and Paul felt gentle hands being laid on him, comforting and reassuring, followed by the words which offered encouragement. "Brother Saul."

The actions and the words told him not to be afraid, that there was no revenge here, no hatred, no gloating. And then Ananias

"People are looking for acceptance and love"

informed him of God's intentions.

We live in a world where people are quick to hate and seek revenge. Where sometimes, in the case of those who have done terrible things and then repent, we feel it's not fair, that they should be made to pay for the things that they've done.

Ananias might have felt the same way about Paul, but he went in faith and showed the love of Christ in those two words.

"Brother Saul."

"The vilest offender who truly believes, that moment from Jesus a pardon receives," the hymn says.

The parable of the workers in the vineyard reminds us that there are workers being hired at the last hour of the day and that they will be paid the same wage as us.

People are looking for acceptance and love. When we have been forgiven ourselves and know the love of Christ, when we are being obedient to what God wants, then we can be loving and gentle and offer the hand of fellowship to others. ■

Word Of
Wisdom

By Rev. Ian W.F. Hamilton

IT'S not often that I make one single word the focus of "From The Manse Window", but on this occasion I wish to do so as Lent comes around again in the Christian calendar.

The word I wish to speak about isn't one that will immediately strike you as being a "wealthy" word.

There are so many words in the New Testament which are wealthy in meaning – words like redemption, grace, sin, repentance, forgiveness.

But the word I have in mind is in no way comparable in terms of richness. Instead, it is a word which is merely used to link sentences together.

That word is "nevertheless".

Let's at the outset be clear about its meaning.

It is described in the dictionary as equivalent to "notwithstanding" or "although". It's the conjunction which introduces a qualification or an exception.

So it really is a word that suggests that there is more than one point of view, that there are always two sides to any matter or to any question!

Long ago, Jesus used the word himself to illustrate that not only does a question have two sides to it, but that a prayer has two sides to it as well!

Prayer isn't only a case of asking, of petition. It is also a case of submission, that is, submitting to God's will.

When Jesus saw the Cross on the horizon and became aware of all the suffering that this would entail – something we think about especially during Lent – he said a prayer to God in which, really, he was begging a favour.

iStock.

He prayed in the following words: "Father, if it be possible, let this cup pass from me; nevertheless, not as I will but as you will."

Jesus begged that he might be spared the anguish ahead. After all, Jesus was human like you and me, and he desperately wanted to avoid the pain and suffering he knew without doubt was coming.

But, unlike you and me, perhaps, Jesus was prepared to accept also that God was much wiser than he was.

And so, following on from that very human cry of desperation, Jesus went on to say, "Nevertheless, let your will be done."

Now, of course, we have all said prayers like this, especially when we are up against it.

But Jesus realised that there was the other side to the situation – and that was God's view of it.

He prayed he would be released from the agonies to come on the Cross.

He wasn't, but he was given the strength and the power to endure those agonies.

His petition, what he was asking for, was refused, but his prayer was answered nevertheless.

Of course, from all of this an important conclusion follows – it means we know that that no prayer of ours will ever go unanswered.

Certainly, the petition may be refused – God knows best – but the prayer will be answered.

Whenever you are up against it, may you know your prayers to be answered, and may you each be given the strength and the power to overcome these situations, nevertheless. ∎

Strength In
Numbers

By Kathrine Davey, Mansfield Methodist preacher

A **FEW** days ago I was asked to speak at a church that was closing. As I sat down to prepare my talk, I found myself wondering what to say. After all, it was a tangible reminder of the decline of church-going in this country, and hardly a cause for great celebrations.

I had many memories from my childhood of this church, and I realised I was not the only one – for the number of people who attended to mark its passing far exceeded the numbers who attended weekly.

So many of them had a story to tell, of how the long-departed members of this church had made such a difference in their lives. A lot of them had travelled here with a single aim in mind – to be able to wallow in nostalgia – and I was among them.

I said that it would be interesting to find how many of the regular attenders were still attending a church in a few years' time. Although, in many ways we don't have to worry, because Jesus has already said, "I will build my church". By this I don't think he meant the building, although over the years people have built some very impressive buildings which they dedicated to the glory of God.

Rather, he saw "church" as being about the people who lived according to his laws and were continually worshipping God. This means that belief will continue even if the buildings where we learned about this belief are gone.

Many church buildings are

iStock.

increasingly "multi-purpose". That is, they meet in schools or community centres. Even the buildings that are designated as "churches" run many activities that serve the locality, such as toddler groups, pre-schools and luncheon clubs. In fact, churches seem to be going back to the "original design" in the book of the Acts of the Apostles, where groups of people met in someone's house, or in a community building, and eventually grew large enough to feel they could take on the name of "church". Purpose-built church buildings came later.

But in my talk I gave the warning that that doesn't mean that believers are meant to go it alone. I could not decide for each person what church they should become a member of. Yet I urged them to find Christian fellowship with others.

The Bible makes it clear that belief survives best in communities. We are often told that we must learn to live in unity and Christians have a God-given duty to encourage each other. How can we show unity among us or encourage each other if there is no-one else there?

If you have a coal fire, you will notice that all the pieces of coal remain hot and produce sparks while they are together, but the minute a coal is removed from the others, the glow disappears from it, and it soon becomes cooler. So it is with faith. If we determine to live without a Christian community, then we might find that our faith goes "off the boil", too.

Of course, there are examples throughout history of Christians being alone and having no others around to help them sustain their faith. But these are exceptions, and are often people who have a very firm foundation and have built up a close relationship with God.

It is important for us all to build firm foundations for our faith, especially as there are so many things around that challenge our beliefs. Christ often gives us his help through others. ■

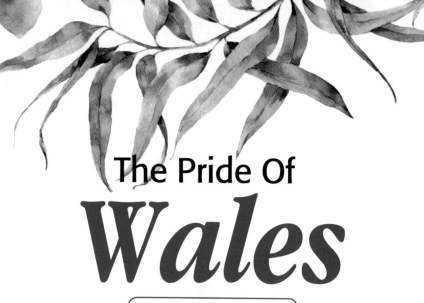

The Pride Of
Wales

By Rev. Ian W.F. Hamilton

IT is on March 1 that many Welsh men and women take great pride in wearing either a leek or a daffodil, because that date celebrates St David's Day. St David, as many will know, is the patron saint of Wales, the leek is the Welsh National Emblem and the daffodil is the country's national flower.

The red dragon is prominent on the Flag of Wales and it, too, is a popular Welsh symbol along with the Tudor colours of green and white on that flag.

Our history books tell us that this flag was used by Henry VII at the Battle of Bosworth in 1485, after which it was carried in state to St Paul's Cathedral in London. The red dragon was subsequently included in the Tudor royal arms to signify their Welsh descent, and in 1959 it was recognised officially as the Welsh national flag.

The leek, the country's national emblem, is associated with their patron saint, David. Apparently David ordered his Welsh soldiers to identify themselves by wearing a vegetable on their helmets during an ancient battle that took place against the Saxons, which happened to be fought in a leek field!

The daffodil tradition is related to the disciple Peter, as in Welsh the daffodil is known as "Peter's Leek".

So now you know!

Wherever Welshmen gather, and particularly in the Welsh Army Regiments, there are countless leeks to be seen, especially on St David's Day!

However, the strikingly obvious

iStock.

question follows: who was St David? David is the English form of his name, but the Welsh equivalent is "Dewi".

Dewi Sant, it is said, was born in the south-west corner of Wales which is known today as Pembrokeshire. Indeed, St David's Cathedral today stands on the site of the monastery he founded in the Glyn Rhosyn valley of Pembrokeshire.

Comparatively little is known about his early life, but it is clear that he pledged himself to the service of Jesus by building this monastery. During his lifetime he founded no fewer than 12 monasteries throughout Great Britain.

Some records tell us that he went on a long journey to Jerusalem and that there the church made him a bishop. At home in Wales he did meet some opposition, but generally he was very well liked and eventually he became an archbishop.

St David is remembered in the cathedral and in the city today, both of which bear his name, as well as in the hearts of Welsh men and women throughout the world.

None of us may ever have founded a monastery, or have become a bishop or an archbishop, and none of us may ever have had a city or a cathedral named after us. However, the one thing we can have in common with St David is that we, too, can pledge our lives to loving and serving Jesus Christ.

Whether we are St David, or just David, St Andrew, or just Andrew – or John or Gary or Julie or Caroline – we are all equally important to Jesus.

Because he loves us all and, as we give our lives to the service of his church, he helps us, of that we can be absolutely sure!

Jesus never calls us into his service and leaves us on our own. Remember his promise.

"I will be with you always."

We can learn so much from the great saints who have gone before us, like Wales's St David, but the greatest lesson of all that they teach us is to commit our lives to the faithful, joyful service of Jesus Christ. ∎

Stormy

Weather

By Rev. Ian Petrie

"E VERYWHERE you go, always take the weather with you," sung by Crowded House, must rank as my favourite line of a pop song ever. The question, I suppose, is this: do we have a choice other than to take the weather with us, wherever we go?

Of course we can always escape from our dreich weather here to the sunshine elsewhere, but that solution is not foolproof, far less waterproof! How often do we hear that the rain has poured in the Mediterranean while we have basked in sunshine on the North Sea coast?

The state of the weather features prominently in our daily chatter, doesn't it? We greet strangers with a cheery "Fine day", or, more often, a glum "Cold today."

Talking about the weather is a popular way of breaking the ice, so to speak, when all other subjects fail. Our wide variety of weather is well described as "four seasons in one day"!

It is this variety which gives our countryside its rich colour, much-admired beauty and a fertility which produces abundant harvests.

Opinions vary as to what constitutes good and bad weather. The people of the Bible experienced very different weather conditions from ours and so had a different perspective on good and bad weather days.

"As the rain and snow come down from heaven" was a forecast through the prophet Isaiah from the Lord. "And do not return to it without watering the earth and making it bud and flourish, so that it yields seed for the sower and bread to eat, so the word that goes from my mouth will not return to

iStock.

me empty."

So, in many areas of our world, rain and even snow would turn out to be very good weather indeed!

One person who knew all about the weather was Noah. He was so convinced that floods were imminent that he set about building an Ark, much to the amusement of his mocking neighbours.

Noah's conviction never wavered as he laboured away beneath the sun-baked blue sky, because we are told that "he walked with God and did everything that he commanded" and God had forecast very stormy weather, featuring the flood to end all floods.

Noah, his family and two of every species of beast entered his

completed Ark and, after a week of rising winds and gathering storm clouds, the floods arrived with a vengeance and stayed for over six weeks.

The rain stopped and the flood level went down over a period of a further three weeks, until Noah sent a dove from the Ark for a weather check. No dry land meant the dove's return. There was a further week's delay before the dove returned a second time, bearing a freshly plucked olive leaf.

Noah, his family and every beast disembarked on to dry land and Noah started building again, this time an altar in thanksgiving to God.

Then there came a momentous weather forecast of sunshine and showers. It produced a rainbow, designated by God as the everlasting sign of his covenant promise through Noah to "every living thing that is found on earth, for ever".

Noah walked with God, we're told, travelling wherever God's weather took him. In the words of another pop song, he was to discover that "the answer, my friend is blowing in the wind; the answer is blowing in the wind." ■

Let There Be
Light

By Rev. David Bryant

WE would be lost today without electricity in our homes. Every street has its electrically powered gadgets. There are vacuum cleaners, television, radios, fridges, freezers, washing machines and dishwashers all whizzing away doing their job.

Add to that immersion heaters, electric fires, music systems, DIY tools and electric lights and you see how heavily dependent we are on electric power. I would be lost without it, for I still use a sturdy office electric typewriter that must be all of thirty-five years old. It is an old friend I would not wish to be without.

When I was a boy, life was very different. My first memories are of living in a rambling Victorian vicarage that had no electricity laid on. Cooking was done on a blackleaded range, there was no central heating and hot water was provided by a coke-fired boiler.

Worst of all, there were no electric lights. The house was lit by oil lamps which took a great deal of looking after. They had to be filled regularly, the wicks needed constant adjustment and trimming and they emitted an unpleasant smell.

They were not ideal for a child, because on winter evenings the house was full of shadows and pockets of darkness, and it was creepy. Even the nightlight that was left burning in the nursery did not

iStock.

melt away the gloom.

What a transformation there was when electricity came to the vicarage! You could enter a dark room, push down the brass switch and fill the space with light. Other pieces of equipment began to appear.

My father purchased a new wireless on which he could listen to the war news. A gramophone appeared one day, with a wind-up handle and needles that went blunt and had to be sharpened in a special device that consisted of a revolving disc of sandpaper. An electric cooker was installed in the kitchen and electric fires took the chill off icy bedrooms.

Electricity means light and power and it is easy to see why Christ is referred to in the New Testament as the Light of the World, the one who conquers all that is dark and wrong. The opening verses of the Book of Genesis used the same image.

"And God said, 'Let there be light', and there was light. And God saw that the light was good: and God separated the light from the darkness."

But the idea is taken a step further. Followers of Christ are called on to show light in the world and to live lives that glow out with love, joy, compassion and kindness. As Christ says in the Sermon on the Mount, "Let your light so shine before men that they may see your good works and give glory to your Father who is in heaven."

It is something worth remembering the next time you switch on the bedroom light. ∎

A farmer often stopped to watch his cattle lazing around chewing the cud. They seemed at peace with themselves and their calmness transferred to him, he said. They had not a care in the world and, thereafter, neither did he! Try it the next time you see a field of cows!

Let Me
Serve You

By Kathrine Davey, Mansfield Methodist preacher

WHEN I was young I had a pet rabbit. I loved that rabbit very much and did my best to look after its every need. One day I decided he was hungry, and I was determined to find something suitable.

However, instead of some juicy dandelion leaves, I looked around and the only thing nearby was a sandpit. So I decided that would do. I didn't realise that sand is not on the list of healthy foods for rabbits and the inevitable happened – suffice to say I never had another rabbit!

Although I had done something that had terrible consequences (especially for the rabbit, as nobody had ever explained to me that rabbits do not eat sand), my motives were very good as I was determined to act to settle the problem immediately.

My parents realised that I had learned a lesson from the incident, and knew that I had not set out to injure the rabbit.

There is often a similar dilemma when we have to decide if we will act with the risk of regretting it later, or live with the regret of not acting at all. If we never act, we run the risk of becoming known as indecisive and not being useful to anyone.

There are many lonely people in the world whose greatest need is to be of use to someone. They would echo John Wesley's prayer, "Lord, let me not live to be useless".

Jesus understood the human need to help each other and do a service for others, as he often asked others for help. He met a Samaritan woman at a well, so John's gospel tells us, and before engaging her in conversation, he

iStock.

asked for her help in giving him a drink of water. Jesus often stayed at other people's houses, and so he expected them to look after him.

When Jesus meets the tax-collector Zacchaeus who was hiding in a tree, his first words are to ask him to come down because "I must stay at your house today".

Zacchaeus was a member of an unpopular profession, often accused of being "less than honest with his expenses". Things are not so different today, yet this story shows us that Jesus would undoubtedly have approached these modern wrongdoers.

These two incidents where Jesus asks a favour have in common the surprise caused by his request. The Samaritan woman seems to have led an immoral life, and certainly came to the well at a time of day when she would avoid any disapproving contact with the rest of her community.

The crowd saw Jesus and Zacchaeus walking together and there was a general murmur of disapproval that he had gone to be the guest of a "sinner".

Jesus often approaches other people and shows his interest in them by asking them to do a favour. His disciples must have been used to being needed by him, and on several occasions he calls on their help.

On Palm Sunday, he sends two of them to fetch the donkey needed for his entry into Jerusalem, and a few days later, when he institutes the sacrament of the Last Supper, he tells his followers to make preparations for the meal.

There is a modern hymn that puts it beautifully:

"Brother, sister, let me serve you,
Let me be as Christ to you . . ."

Jesus is the perfect example of unselfish behaviour, and following his example may have unexpected benefits.

The Bible tells us that we should be prepared to show hospitality to anybody, even strangers, "for by so doing some people have shown hospitality to angels without knowing it".■

The True
Message

By Rev. Dr James Martin

THE English language contains many remarkable features. Not the least interesting of these is the manner in which identical phrases can carry the exact opposite meaning when used in different contexts. A very stirring example of this phenomenon is provided by the Bible in its report of the last words spoken by Jesus before he died on the cross.

"It is finished." (John 19:30)

This was initially understood by everyone to be an admission of final defeat, a recognition by Jesus that he had failed in his mission, which was ending not in success, but in failure.

"The game's up. It's all over." That was the message his words conveyed to all who were interested. Whatever enterprise Jesus had been engaged upon was now over, without its purpose being achieved.

His disciples were broken-hearted and concerned now with saving their own selves, waiting only for the Sabbath to be over and its travel restrictions to be removed so that they could go back home to nurse their regrets.

The enemies of Jesus, for their part – the Pharisees and the rest – were rejoicing that this troublesome pest was no more. It was "finished".

But then came the resurrection of Jesus and the true meaning of "It is finished" became plain. Jesus's mission had in fact been completed. His work of salvation had been truly finished, in the sense of being completely accomplished.

What had appeared to be dismal

iStock.

defeat was now revealed to be glorious victory, not only for Jesus himself but also for all who would choose to trust and follow him.

I remember going in my student days to see a much-heralded sculpture by Epstein entitled "Consummatum Est" ("It is finished"). It was a massive figure of the dead Jesus.

Young Christian that I was, and unaware of what might have been in Epstein's mind and heart, I was appalled at what struck me as the apparent desolate hopelessness of that lifeless carved figure of Jesus. It seemed to me to give not the slightest hint of that dead figure able to rise to life.

I was moved to recall a true story I had recently come across about Wellington's victory at the Battle of Waterloo. A group of interested politicians had arranged for a ship to bring news of the battle to them as they waited at a vantage point on the south coast of England.

Eventually the awaited ship came into view and dropped anchor close to shore. The signaller began to spell out his message letter by letter: "W-E-L-L-I-N-G-T-O-N D-E-F-E-A-T-E-D . . ."

Just then a blanket of fog descended to hide the ship from sight. The watchers on shore were desolate at what seemed to have been a disastrous outcome of the battle. A number of them were too stricken to leave and were still there when the fog cleared and the signaller was seen to complete his message – "Wellington defeated the enemy."

Apparent defeat was, after all, glorious victory, and that is, of course, the Gospel message. The crucified Jesus is risen and alive, offering victory in living and even over death, to all who decide to trust and follow him. Good news, indeed, the very best. ∎

The Symbols Of
Love

By Rev. David Bryant

THE weeks leading up to Easter Day were always a favourite with our children when they were small.

The reason was simple – there were always all sorts of delicious, special foods to eat, all made in the vicarage kitchen by my wife.

The feast started on Shrove Tuesday, also known as Pancake Day. The batter was mixed by the boys with wooden spoons and the mixture poured into a frying-pan. Tossing them was always a hit or miss business and sometimes one landed on the floor, to the accompaniment of groans.

The next treat was sticky hot cross buns. They were very popular at elevenses time and they were even more tasty when toasted and spread with butter and jam.

Another food greeted with enthusiasm was the Easter simnel cake which was made from lemon, dried fruit peel, treacle and grilled marzipan paste.

Usually simnel cakes are decorated with eleven balls of marzipan in a circle with an extra one in the middle. Sometimes we used to cook a very large one and take it to church. After the service every member of the congregation would enjoy a slice.

Not surprisingly, topping the list came Easter eggs. In the 1800s these were hardboiled hens' eggs painted in pretty colours. By 1875 shops were selling chocolate versions.

iStock.

Each food has a Christian message. Pancakes were eaten on Shrove Tuesday, the last day before the fasting season of Lent, when Christians would give up something or nowadays are more likely try to give extra to charity or help a neighbour or sick person at a difficult time. It was the last chance to enjoy the richness of eggs, sugar and butter before Lent began.

Hot cross buns have a cross piped on top of them. They were originally known as Good Friday buns, and were eaten on that day and no other. They are a reminder to us of how Jesus died on the cross for our sins.

The eleven marzipan balls on a simnel cake represent eleven of the disciples, leaving out Judas Iscariot, the twelfth. The single ball in the middle stands for Christ.

The word simnel comes from the Latin *simila*, meaning white, and refers to the special pure flour used in the cooking. In Victorian times young girls in service took a simnel cake home to their mothers as a present.

Easter eggs are a symbol of the Resurrection of Jesus. A bird hatches from the egg, leaving behind it a shell or empty tomb. In this same way Jesus rose from the grave, leaving it a rocky, bare cave.

In AD 1610 the Christian church officially came to see Easter eggs as a symbol of resurrection and used this prayer.

"Bless, O Lord, we beseech thee, this thy creature of eggs, that it may become a wholesome sustenance to thy faithful servants, eating it in thankfulness to thee on account of the resurrection of the Lord."

Therefore, not only are the Easter foods a delicious treat to enjoy, they also remind us of the God who is all love and compassion. ■

Picking Up The
Pieces

By Rev. Ian Petrie

WE all have the odd cringeworthy moment, don't we? I can choose from a wide variety, spread over the years.

Here is one, brought to mind at a recent coffee morning by a full cup being knocked over. Its contents spilled, but the cup itself remained unbroken. Mine was not so lucky!

I can't remember the year, but certainly will not forget the occasion. Scotland were playing England at Wembley, and I had just settled down to watch the match.

We were staying at my parents' home in Arbroath as part of our holiday with our young family, and my mother had just poured me a cup of tea, with an oft-repeated warning to be careful "as the cup and saucer were made of china"!

Heedless of her advice, I balanced cup and saucer on the arm of my chair – no doubt out of sheer bad habit.

The next moment Scotland scored and I leaped up from my chair. My rising left arm caught my cup and saucer as cleanly as Gordon McQueen had his marvellous header moments earlier.

There was a moment's stunned silence.

My mother then fixed me with an "I told you so" stare; Marion, my wife, looked totally embarrassed, and the kids wore an expectant look.

Clearly they were wondering

iStock.

what was going to happen next. Their dad, used to telling them off, was now well and truly in trouble himself!

"I'm very sorry," I blurted out, "but Scotland scored!" As if that was anywhere near an excuse.

Speechless with fury, my mother went looking for a cloth while Marion helped me to pick up the shattered pieces of the china cup and saucer. The situation wasn't helped by England's equalising goal!

Every negative has a positive, including broken crockery.

"God sets the time for tearing," Ecclesiastes preaches in chapter three, "and the time for mending."

While having the sense not to make this suggestion at the time, I thought of another cup, one of a family set which had borne the name *IAN*.

This cup had been shattered, far beyond the possibility of any mending. Even the letters of my name had been ripped apart into multiple jigsaw pieces.

Something made me keep the pieces, as a mirror of the broken IAN that is myself.

"Now we see only puzzling reflections in a mirror," Paul wrote to Corinth, "but then we shall see face to face."

Is it possible that we will see beyond the brokenness to being mended and becoming whole again? We have all broken something, haven't we? And had feelings of brokenness?

Crockery can be broken, as can hearts and promises. Once shattered, crockery can never be completely mended. But can we?

Among Jesus's most moving words are, "This is my body, broken for you," as he breaks the bread. "Do this in remembrance of me."

It is wonderful to remember that, through the very act of sharing his broken body, we make it one again. ■

The Bare
Necessities

By Rev. Andrew Watson

SOME things are easy enough for us to say. The words roll off our tongues before we know it – "Don't worry, it will be all right!"

We mean well. Our wishes are sincere and with all our hearts we want to believe it.

But when we wake in the wee small hours with a hospital appointment, an interview or an exam the next day, we don't feel quite so confident, do we? Our palms can't help sweating, our pulse races and our stomach won't stop tying itself in knots.

Will the children remember all that stuff they revised? Will that job work out? Will the doctor give us good news? Or even more basic worries?

As circumstances of life inevitably change, will we have enough to make ends meet? Will it really be all right?

We could listen to the advice given by laid-back bear Baloo to the young "man-cub" Mowgli in Disney's popular movie "The Jungle Book":

"Don't spend your time looking around

"For something you want that can't be found.

"When you find out you can live without it

"And go along not thinking about it,

"I tell you something true –

"The bare necessities of life will come to you!"

Wise advice from a cartoon character! And sometimes that's how it seems.

Out of the blue, when we least expect it, when we weren't even consciously seeking it, along comes something that turns out

iStock.

to be just what we need. A kind offer of help. A generous gift. A surprise opportunity. Some encounter with a friend or stranger that gives us the encouragement to continue. We find what we need to get by.

These things don't happen by random chance. Behind the gifts there is a Giver. Behind the provision there is a gracious and generous Provider, our Father in heaven, who causes sun and rain to fall on both good and wicked people and delights in giving good gifts to his children.

This was one of Jesus's themes in his Sermon on the Mount.

"Do not worry about your life, what you will eat or drink; or about your body, what you will wear . . . Do not worry about tomorrow, for tomorrow will worry about itself. Each day has enough trouble of its own!" (Matthew 6:25, 34.)

Jesus urges his followers to look at the birds and wildflowers. Our Father feeds and clothes them. He'll look after us even better if we seek his kingdom and righteousness as our first priority.

He will ensure we get the things he knows we need.

Think of the imagery of the 23rd Psalm.

The Lord, our kind Shepherd, will lead us to good, safe pasture and quiet, refreshing waters. Jesus acknowledges that in this world we will have our share of trouble and sorrow, but he will comfort us in the valley of shadow, and even prepare a table of fine food to sustain us when facing our enemies!

He has laid down his life for us that we might be brought safe home, eventually to "dwell in the house of the Lord for ever".

Thus the Apostle Paul, when facing trials and even mortal danger, could write, "The Lord is near. Do not be anxious about anything, but in everything, by prayer . . . with thanksgiving, present your requests to God. And the peace of God, which transcends all understanding, will guard your hearts and your minds in Christ Jesus." (Philippians 4:5-7.) ■

> ## "Behind the gifts there is a Giver"

Do You
Remember?

By Kathrine Davey, Mansfield Methodist preacher

A **QUICK** quiz for you all. According to the skipping rhyme, what did my mother say that you should never do?

If you know the answer to this question then I am sure you would have fitted in well with the nostalgia evening held by our ladies' group at church recently. Many of the clapping games or skipping rhymes that we recited, which were so familiar to many generations, were team games, open to all.

As I recall, the number of children in each team was always "flexible" to allow all who wanted to join in. The skipping-rope was often long enough to accommodate several skippers, and there were always plenty of bystanders. The familiar words meant that even people new to the area were able to participate and were not left as outsiders.

There were regional variations of the same game with different words or rules. For example, It or Tig or Tag (or other names) had a variety of ways of deciding how someone was "out". But wherever it was played, you were never out of the game for long. And I mustn't ignore you gentlemen readers, who probably remember using your jumpers as impromptu goalposts for a game of football, or the rowdy games of British Bulldog that took over the playground.

I'm sure that Jesus's disciples had their own "nostalgia evening" after they found that the person they had given up so much to follow had been killed. Their memories were probably on the lines of, "Do you remember when we did such and such a thing with him?"

After all, they had given up several years of their lives to follow him, and so now all they thought

iStock.

they were left with was memories. They were there and had witnessed first-hand when Jesus calmed the storm, fed over 5,000 people and healed the sick.

But now they were certain he was gone, and for a while they just had the rest of their group to make sure that their disappointment was not allowed to turn into resentment at such a waste, or even bitterness that Jesus had betrayed their hopes in him.

Despite their differences and disagreements, I am sure that Jesus knew that a group of people would be able to encourage and support each other, just as he knew that difficulties would occur.

When they met their living Lord, on that first Easter day, he proved that their sense of nostalgia was not wasted, for their memories of him helped them to understand the things that were to come. After all, he had told them what was to happen to him several times before his death. It was only when they looked back at his words made sense.

In fact, it was this nostalgia for the things that Jesus said and did while he was alive that caused the gospel accounts to be written, so that those of us who weren't there would have some record of what happened. But there are four gospels, all written by someone different, and so each giving an individual slant on what happened.

I don't suppose they realised, when they were in the depths of despair, that this team of ordinary working men that Jesus had built up around him were to become famous as storytellers, nor that their stories would be translated into many languages.

Like those playground games, it occurred to me then that Christianity is a bit of a team game. We all need each other at times, to help us or encourage us on life's journey.

It seems to me that there is often not enough appreciation of the others in our team, whose job is to prompt those who have forgotten to tell the others not to play in the wood! ■

An Ever-open
Door

(**By Rev. Dr James Martin**)

I**N** an idle moment the other day I selected a volume from my bookshelf with the title "And Jesus Said". It is a book written by the famous expositor of the Christian Gospel, Professor William Barclay.

It contains his exposition of the parables of Jesus and, despite its age, is still very much up to date in what it says about these stories that Jesus employed in his preaching. I was struck by the words I read on the first page.

"Even in an age where people know less and less about the Bible, and care less for it, the stories Jesus told are the best-known stories in the world."

Whether or not we reckon this statement to be as valid as it was when written, it is beyond doubt that the parables of Jesus are still

very widely known. One of the best known is undoubtedly the one about the Prodigal Son (Luke 15:11-32).

Readers are sure to know this story already. The younger son of a well-to-do man of property became unhappy with the disciplines of home and decided he would be much happier to cut himself free of them.

He went to his father and asked that the one-third portion of the estate which would by law come to him on his father's demise be given to him now.

Hurt though he was by this selfish request, the father consented and the son went off far away, to squander his fortune in wild and immoral activities. Finding himself destitute and sinking deeper and deeper into life's mire,

the prodigal came to his senses and decided to crawl back home to meet the condemnation he was expecting to receive but hoping that his father, having first rebuked him, might find him some menial job.

To his astonishment and joy his father, who had never stopped loving him despite his delinquency, welcomed him with open arms and restored him to the body of the family.

By means of this parable Jesus is telling us that he never stops loving us, no matter how far we might wander away from him or let him down, and is always ready to welcome us back when we come to our senses and return to him.

The Gospel record actually tells us of Jesus affirming this very thing in John 6:37 – "I will never turn anyone away who comes to me."

This ever-open door of his is one of the many sure facts of the Gospel, and a wonderful one it is. But there is real danger of some people choosing to shut that door against themselves. The Gospel narratives tell of a few who flirted with that danger.

There is Nicodemus, for one. Pharisee that he was, although impressed by Jesus in his early acquaintance with him, Nicodemus had some serious theological doubts, particularly concerning Jesus's claim that people could have their sins forgiven and their lives transformed through faith in him.

Happily, although the Bible does not record the how and when of it, Nicodemus did come to enter through Jesus's open door so that we find him as a believer helping to bury Jesus after his crucifixion (John 3:1-13 and 19:39-42).

Many refuse to come to Jesus's open door, for different reasons – perhaps fearing ridicule from friends, perhaps thinking their sins rule them out, or because of something else.

But Jesus has that door always open and it is there for everyone who chooses to use it. ■

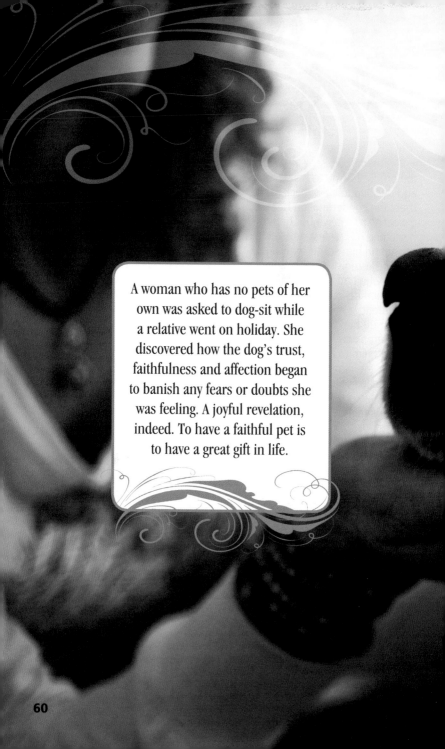

A woman who has no pets of her own was asked to dog-sit while a relative went on holiday. She discovered how the dog's trust, faithfulness and affection began to banish any fears or doubts she was feeling. A joyful revelation, indeed. To have a faithful pet is to have a great gift in life.

Hidden

Treasure

By Rev. Barbara Mosse

iStock.

AST winter I found myself thinking of one of those long-ago childhood summers on holiday at one of our favourite places – Port Erin on the Isle of Man.

On a particular day in 1971 my sister and I had spent many happy hours on the beach. We had run in and out of the warm water and we had built sandcastles. What next?

"Let's clamber over those rocks and explore the cave behind them. Maybe we'll find some buried treasure!"

With our parents' permission, Sheila and I set out on our adventure.

The rocks were dry and warm, pitted with rock pools left by the retreating tide. In no time we were standing at the mouth of the cave.

The pebbles around us were bathed in sunshine, but beyond the first few feet the back of the cave was shrouded in darkness. We started digging, scooping up the multi-coloured stones. I got side-tracked by their beauty and variety, so it wasn't surprising that Sheila was the first to strike gold – well, one old penny, actually.

She held it up triumphantly. Then she found another, and another. Within a few minutes we had a sixpence, two threepenny bits, two more pennies and six halfpennies between us.

We scrambled back to our parents, who thought someone must have left his trousers in the cave while he went for a swim, and

managed to lose the change in his pockets.

Bank notes, if we found them in the street, we would hand in at a police station. But Dad thought it unlikely that anyone would come back to the cave looking for such a small sum, so we were allowed to keep our findings.

Jesus offered his disciples two short parables about hidden treasure, and they are found paired together in Matthew's gospel.

"The kingdom of heaven is like treasure hidden in a field, which someone found and hid; then in his joy he goes and sells all that he has and buys that field. Again, the kingdom of heaven is like a merchant in search of fine pearls; on finding one pearl of great value, he went and sold all that he had and bought it".
(Matthew 13:44-45.)

There are big differences between our experience of finding "treasure" and the treasure Jesus talks about. Someone once said that God's gift to us – his kingdom, his love – is free, but it isn't cheap. Both the person who finds the treasure in a field and the merchant who finds the pearl sell all they have in order to buy the treasure.

We can't buy God's love in that way, but if we've chosen to follow him we will know that it does cost us – in terms of love and commitment, and a willingness to trust God's will as we live our daily lives.

I can't remember what Sheila and I spent our bounty on, but I suspect it didn't last us very long!

There's another difference between our experience and Jesus's teaching about God's kingdom. Sheila and I didn't have to sell anything to buy our treasure, and although our pleasure was great, the effects were short-lived.

In contrast, the treasure God offers asks for our love and commitment, and its effects will last for all eternity. ■

God's Call To
Change

By Rev. Susan Sarapuk

AT some stage I'll have to replace my computer now that Microsoft has stopped supporting Windows XP. I've only just got used to the one I have after seven years, so I'm filled with trepidation. Many of us don't like change, particularly as we get older.

Our parish church has been through a lot of physical changes in the past couple of years – a new meeting room and kitchen, and the replacement of pews with comfortable chairs – of which I approved. But I have to admit I had to swallow the day I walked in to find the pews gone. That took some getting used to.

Where do we get the notion as Christians that things must always stay the same? We know that God is unchanging, but that refers to his nature. In reality he challenges us to new things.

The first challenge for Jesus's disciples was to leave behind the security of their lives, their work and families, and venture out into the unknown with him. Although their life with Jesus was exciting, they never knew what was going to happen from one day to the next, which could have been stressful.

Eventually even that must have become routine, so that they settled down into thinking everything was under control. Then Jesus started telling them that he was going to be killed.

"No, this will never happen to you!" Peter says, and in that utterance we sense his concern not

iStock.

64

just for Jesus but also for himself. It's a cry against change.

The biggest upset was the death and then – arguably even more challenging – the resurrection of Jesus, followed weeks later by the coming of the Holy Spirit at Pentecost. How could any of Jesus's disciples have predicted the paths their lives would take? In the end they didn't try to control things; they went where God led them and great things happened because of it.

Perhaps we are scared to trust God in that way. Maybe the world is moving on so fast we want to cling to something that makes us feel secure and doesn't change, and often that's our church. We want to keep it the way it's always been, as a haven in a mad world.

But it is the Lord who is our rock, not our church buildings and the way we worship. We forget that and replace the living God with a devotion to our church, and when he calls us to move on with him we're deaf to that call. Is that why many of our chapels have closed, and why a lot of our churches seem on the brink of going the same way?

I'm not advocating getting rid of the traditional altogether – we still need the great hymns because of the truths they teach us. But a congregation that refuses to do anything new won't attract new converts. Nor must we change doctrine or the commandments or the truths of Christianity, but we do need to change the way we communicate them and the way we relate to people.

We need to be open to the living God because maybe he wants to change us. Maybe he wants to bring a Pentecost experience to our lives; to shake us up, to make us useful, to liberate us from being timid.

I will continue to use my computer, but in time it will grow less effective and be compromised by viruses. What good will it be then? Not fit for purpose. What about our spiritual lives? ■

The Sound Of
Music

By Rev. Ian W.F. Hamilton

THE year 2015 was a significant one in the film world because in March 1965 the immortal film "The Sound Of Music" was released in Hollywood, which means that it celebrated its golden anniversary.

There are few who haven't seen this wonderful film at least twice, and the memorable music and songs of Rodgers and Hammerstein are always a joy to the ear.

So, let's start at the very beginning. It's a very good place to start!

Rarely has a motion picture captured the imagination of the public as has "The Sound Of Music" since its release. It's a film that blends history, music, the picturesque Austrian film location in and around Salzburg, deep and heartfelt emotion and, not least, the lovely voice of Julie Andrews.

It's the story of a young novice who has entered strict Nonnberg Abbey, a handsome Austrian naval captain who lives nearby and 10 singing children.

In the film only seven children are featured, but in the original story of Maria von Trapp, 10 children make up the full family singing complement.

Sister Maria is sent to the von Trapp home as a governess to the children following the death of their mother. She falls in love with the captain and they live happily ever after, at least after their escape from their beloved occupied homeland at the time of World War II.

The story is a real tear-jerker, but anyone who knows their do-re-mis would surely agree that the

iStock.

melodious songs of Rodgers and Hammerstein glue the story together in the closest and deepest of harmonies.

The song "Edelweiss", with its "bless my homeland for ever" message at its heart, was the last song ever to be written by the famous duo. Mistakenly, it has often been thought to be the Austrian National Anthem.

It has to be said that all of the songs from "The Sound Of Music" are winners. Personally speaking, these tunes will be for ever among my favourite things!

It is noticeable, too, that so many of the film's songs have lessons for all of us within them, not least the classic melody sung in the film by Peggy Wood, the Mother Abbess – "Climb Every Mountain".

The song's title is virtually a parable on life. To a large extent life is about climbing mountains – one after the other for some unlucky folks. Mountains of family tragedy, crippling illness or unbelievable misfortune.

"How can we ever get on top of this situation?" many ask.

Mountains can be overpowering at times, and there are no neat, stereotyped answers, I'm afraid, except to say there is a power greater than all the mountainous obstacles that life can ever mete out to us.

"Before the mountains were created," the Psalmist wrote, "before the world was brought into being, you were eternally God . . . and will be God for ever and ever!"

It is in his strength that we must meet and tackle the mountains we each encounter, in the knowledge that he climbs with us "every day of our life for as long as we live" – and even after that when the final mountain has been climbed, crushed and conquered.

Yes, the hills are still alive, and whether you are sixteen going on seventeen, or sixty going on seventy, if you have ears to hear, the sound of music which they echo is none other than the music of the glorious Gospel! ■

Role
Model

By Rev. Andrew Watson

'M generally not a nervous person – I guess you could call me laid back. But as I sat in the Arrivals Meeting Point in Terminal 2 of Dublin Airport I found my pulse starting to quicken in anticipation.

Having checked the noticeboard for the umpteenth time, I stood up and walked to the rail to make sure no-one could go past without me seeing them. Other people were waiting, too.

Some were there to meet strangers for business, with names written on cards. Some were messaging on their phones or yawning, but I was on full alert, leaning forward slightly, my eyes fastened on the automatic doors.

I confess I felt a little choked up and actually had to dab my eyes.

My son was coming home. Our eldest, who had been away for months on a work crew in the States.

The fearless explorer who had been sending us messages and pictures from Mount Rushmore, Graceland Mansion in Memphis, Tennessee, the Hard Rock Café in New Orleans and the mild waters of the Mexican Gulf, to name but a few!

The child I once carried in my arms. The boy I taught to ride a bike and climb. The one who, at times, as a teenager, nearly drove us crazy!

His plane had landed; he was somewhere in the building. And all of a sudden he was there in front of me, bearded and grinning.

With typical Presbyterian reserve

iStock.

we patted each other's backs and exchanged greetings. It was enough.

Inside, my heart was doing happy somersaults. My boy was home, and the party could begin!

I couldn't help but think of Jesus's description of God as a loving father, rejoicing to welcome his child home.

Even in the Old Testament, David could write something of this paternal, loving God.

"The Lord is compassionate and gracious, slow to anger, abounding in love . . . He does not treat us as our sins deserve . . . As a father has compassion on his children, so the Lord has compassion on those who fear him." (Psalm 103:8, 10, 13.)

Jesus underlined this theme and developed it in his Sermon on the Mount, encouraging his followers to pray with humble confidence to God as "Our Father in heaven".

"If you, then, though you are evil, know how to give good gifts to your children," he assured us, "how much more will your Father in heaven give good gifts to those who ask him!" (Matthew 8:11.)

The central message of the New Testament is the "good news" that God loved the world so much he gave his own son in sacrifice, so that those who receive him and believe in his name could become God's children for ever!
(John 1:12.)

As role models, some fathers leave a lot to be desired, with the result that many people grow up feeling unloved and insecure. Some struggle with low self-esteem, or strive to overachieve without any assurance of ever having earned acceptance.

How liberating, then, to discover we don't have to labour to earn our heavenly father's love! He loves us anyway, and always has. He is full of compassion and mercy. He delights to provide for our needs.

And he is waiting eagerly in the Arrivals Lounge to welcome us home! ■

Spreading The
Word

By Rev. Susan Sarapuk

HOW do you do your washing-up? I'm talking to those people who don't have dishwashers, I should say.

A friend of mine was doing the washing-up the other day and he (yes, he) filled the bowl with water first before squirting in the washing-up liquid.

It set him thinking. If you do it that way around you can only wash a couple of things, but if you do it in the traditional way of squirting in the liquid as the bowl is filling up, then you very quickly get a load of bubbles and you can wash everything.

It made me think of the Holy Spirit.

When Jesus was on earth there was a limit to what he could do, and even though, on one occasion,

he sent out 72 followers to heal the sick and announce the coming of the kingdom, that, too, was limited in its effect.

They were confined to one place and a certain number of people.

But when the Spirit came at Pentecost there was no limit to what God could accomplish because there was no longer just Jesus and a handful of disciples to do the work. Every follower was filled with the Spirit and was able to do what Jesus did.

After all, he'd promised that his disciples would do even greater things than him because he was going to the Father.

"I wish I could have lived in the time of Jesus so I could have seen him and witnessed what he did first hand," people often say.

iStock.

In reality, it would have been a painful experience.

The disciples had no understanding of what was really going on and had to go through the horror of losing their friend and master and the subsequent fear of facing the same end themselves.

Would you have wanted that? At least we have the benefit of hindsight; we know what it was all about and we can have a relationship with Jesus knowing that he is triumphant.

When Jesus finally showed himself to Thomas, who'd been absent at the first resurrection appearance, and Thomas declared, "My Lord and my God!" Jesus questioned whether he believed because he had seen.

"Blessed are those who have not seen and yet believe." (John 20:29.)

That's us – we are blessed.

Blessed because we are living in the age of the Spirit, and blessed because we do not have to face the confusion and trauma the disciples did.

We see it all clearly. We understand why Jesus had to die. We have the Scriptures so we can understand how it all fits together.

The washing-up liquid of the Gospel goes a lot further when all of us bear witness, and we can do so because Jesus has sent the Holy Spirit to fill us with joy and conviction, and make us like him.

One of my favourite verses in the Bible is Philippians 1:6.

"He who began a good work in you will bring it to completion."

It reminds me that it's not about me trying as hard as I possibly can, to be good enough for God.

He started the work of salvation in me and by the power of the Holy Spirit he is going to make sure that I get to heaven – even though at times I stumble and fall.

So we all have a part to play in spreading the good news and, because of the Spirit, we don't do it alone. ∎

> "We all have a part to play in spreading the good news"

In All
Weathers

By Rev. David Bryant.

ORGANISING the parish events for the summer months was always a risky and worrying time for us. Would the weather stay dry for the church fair?

Garden parties were even more of a problem. It hardly seemed appropriate to hold one inside in the church hall.

I recall numerous occasions when I had to make a last-minute decision. Inside or outside? Often I was wrong.

One year all the stallholders had to run for shelter to some tall trees overlooking the vicarage garden. It didn't do their produce any good at all.

If it was light drizzle we usually soldiered on with the few visitors brave enough to attend.

All this talk of rain reminds me of St Swithin, whose feast day falls on July 15. He was born in the reign of King Egbert of Wessex and his ordination to the priesthood followed in the year AD 838.

The King appointed him as tutor to his son and Egbert soon became a close friend of his. Later he was appointed Bishop of Winchester.

St Swithin spent much of his ministry tramping the diocese on foot, calling at people's houses and holding banquets for the poor and destitute. He also built and restored many churches in Wessex.

There are many legends concerning St Swithin. My favourite of these legends is the story of an elderly peasant woman who was crossing a bridge over the River Itchen carrying a basketful of

iStock.

hens' eggs.

Some workmen made fun of her and unkindly smashed the eggs. St Swithin allegedly came to the rescue and mended the shells so that she was able to sell them in the market.

St Swithin is best known for a legend about the weather, however. Before he died he asked to be buried in the churchyard of the minster so that "the sweet rain of heaven might fall upon his grave".

He died in AD 862 and there he lay for many years in the churchyard.

When he became a saint, the

monks of Winchester decided to move his body into the cathedral so that he could be buried in a magnificent shrine. The date set for the ceremony was July 15, AD 964.

On that day it just so happened that there was a tremendous storm and a bout of rain that lasted for 40 days.

It was felt to be St Swithin's way of registering his disapproval.

There is an old verse that tells the story:

St Swithin's Day if thou dost rain,
For forty days it will remain.
St Swithin's Day, if thou be fair,
For forty days 'twill rain nae mair.

His shrine in the cathedral was visited by thousands of pilgrims until it was destroyed on the instructions of King Henry VIII.

A Holy Hole was dug out beneath his resting place so that visitors could crawl inside and be close to his bones, which were believed to have healing powers.

A beautiful new shrine was placed in the cathedral in 1962, a permanent reminder of this holy and saintly man. ■

Three In
One

By Rev. Barbara Mosse.

"GOD the Father, God the Son and God the Holy Spirit bless, preserve and keep you."

Three persons in one God – how can this be? Our minds boggle at the seeming impossibility. One of the early Christian creeds contains these words: "The Father incomprehensible, the Son incomprehensible, the Holy Ghost incomprehensible".

I've heard various illustrations used to clarify things. I've used a few of them myself! There's the clover leaf, with three parts on one stem; or ice, water and steam – three forms of the same element.

My own favourite comes from the 12th-century German mystic Hildegard of Bingen. She suggested a lighted candle, which is made up of three distinct elements – a broad yellow outer flame which in turn encloses a purple mid-section and, at the centre, a glowing wick.

All three elements are, and need to be, present together to enable the flame to burn effectively.

The Holy Trinity is not simply a doctrine dreamed up by the Church, but a living, dynamic spiritual reality.

In earlier centuries the people of the Celtic lands understood this. Alexander Carmichael's Scottish collection of ancient hymns and poems known as "Carmina Gadelica" demonstrates an experience of the Trinity as a protective, active presence throughout a person's life:

God (the Father) and Jesus and the Holy Spirit
Be shielding me and saving me,
As Three and as One,

iStock.

By my knee, by my back, by my side,
Each step of the stormy world.
("The Prayer".)

The Trinity didn't just start as an intellectual conundrum, but rather grew gradually out of people's living experience of God.

The creeds then attempted to capture something of that reality.

In my ministry, one question asked quite regularly was this:

"To whom should I pray?"

The words of the traditional blessing we began with makes clear that the three persons of the Trinity are equal, complementary expressions of the one God.

"God the Father, God the Son and God the Holy Spirit bless, preserve and keep you."

My own answer tends to vary according to circumstances.

Overwhelmed by the grandeur of the mountains or filled with joy at the glories of a sunset, my worship turns to God the Father, the creator of the universe and all its wonders.

However, when I am walking alongside someone whose life experience has been particularly bruising, I find myself praying to God the Son.

Jesus identified with human suffering, and the Son of God encourages us to recognise and welcome him in the poor, the dispossessed and misunderstood.

There may be fleeting moments in prayer when I find myself "lost in wonder, love and praise".

When this happens, words seem superfluous. They may become an active hindrance, disrupting a time of silent communion with God.

At such times I become more conscious of God as the Holy Spirit who prays in us at a level far deeper than words, St Paul says in Romans 8:26.

"So let us not fret about our lack of understanding, because the full reality of God's being will always exceed our human ability to grasp.

"Rather, let us ask God to help us grow in our experience of the Trinity in our daily lives, that we may be drawn ever more deeply into that joyous, mutually self-giving relationship of life and love." ■

A man recently had occasion to visit a friend in his place of work. On the wall above his desk was what people call an inspirational poster. It read: "Life works best when we do."

A good thought for employees and bosses alike, wouldn't you say?

iStock.

Ancient And
Modern

By Rev. Susan Sarapuk

LIKE a lot of churches, we've recently lost our full-time organist, and now the vicar has to look around for someone to play the organ every Sunday.

In the daughter church in the parish there hasn't been an organist for a while; a sung service has gone to a said service with hymns, to a service without any hymns.

Singing is a vital part of our worship – it's why many of the newer churches dedicate a lot of worship time to it. Occasionally I've attended a service at one of the big Pentecostal churches with a band out front leading the worship.

Although I've enjoyed it, I've found myself frequently thinking of how sad it would be if we lost the great old hymns. They teach us a lot about doctrine. Something like

Wesley's "And Can It Be" thrills the soul as the words sink in and you realise they are true, not only as a statement of doctrine, but also in your own life.

"My chains fell off, my heart was free, I rose, went forth and followed thee."

The joy as those words register!

"Bold I approach the eternal throne, and claim the crown, through Christ, my own." As I sing these words I find myself reflecting on the wonder that that is going to be true – and the grace and mercy of God that it can be true!

I imagine being in God's presence with Christian friends who have walked the road of faith with me for over 30 years. How we will look at each other in recognition and joy, and then gaze in awe

iStock.

upon God himself.

Granted, there are modern hymnwriters who have the ability to incorporate doctrine into their lyrics. And you can get that sense from singing choruses, too, as they are meant to bring us into the presence of God. But let's not lose the doctrine.

Although I was sent to Sunday School as a child, I didn't regularly attend church on a Sunday, so when, as a student, I had a conversion experience, I had to learn a lot of hymns from scratch as well as studying the Bible.

It would be sad to lose that rich tradition because we are losing organists and thus no longer sing in our services, or because new songs are dominating our worship.

The other thing I've noticed is how the language of some hymns is being changed. I've written before of how "For All The Saints" has been sanitised, with the removal of all battle references even though the Bible clearly tells us we're in a battle "not against flesh and blood but against the principalities and powers".

However, if we expunge those references from our hymnology then we lose a fundamental part of Christian doctrine.

So my plea is to keep the old hymns alive. I've chosen my favourites for my funeral. Yes, there's one modern one – "In Christ Alone". But then I've gone for "Crown Him With Many Crowns", "At The Name Of Jesus" and "I Cannot Tell", because as well as praising Jesus they are packed with doctrine which should make the singer think and respond.

There is room for all sorts of worship in our churches and all sorts of different songs and hymns. Let's make sure we don't lose any along the way. ■

The Miracle Of
Growth

By Rev. Ian Petrie

GARDENING has never been my favourite hobby, which is unfortunate as manses tend to have large gardens.

Our first manse, in East Kilbride, was a modern house with an unmanageable garden twice the size of any other in the estate.

Its clay soil broke two garden spades and bent the prongs of one fork, all in our first year there. Most of it reverted to grass with the texture of a field rather than a lawn.

Our second manse was a stone building in Dundee with a much more manageable garden and, as a bonus, rich and fertile soil.

However, that magnificent manse view came at the cost of its being set on a hill, with its garden sloping so steeply that it was subsiding.

Rocks had been inserted

strategically to shore up the soil, but the force was such that the rocks were moving, too. Some parts of the rocky garden were inaccessible for fear of avalanche!

Before and after living in manses with a garden, we'd lived in flats without one in Aberdeen and Anstruther. Now, perversely, I was amazed to discover I missed my gardens!

They provide fascinating habitats for a host of living things, not all of them welcome. I loved planting vegetable seeds and was thrilled by the miracle of their growth, only to be disappointed that the fruits of my labour and nature's mystery were harvested by massed armies of insects before me!

Now living in a flat in Edinburgh, I find myself with a compact garden,

iStock.

populated by a wide variety of weeds to the exclusion of anything else!

Portion by portion I dug the garden, weeding as I went and turning over its receptive soil.

The nearby convenience store was selling its remaining bedding plants. I bought a tray of marigolds and got one of pansies free! I added the last tray of geraniums left in the shop, more out of sympathy than anything else.

With a minimum of planning, I planted the marigolds, the pansies and the geraniums, watered them, made a cup of coffee and sat and watched them grow.

Within a couple of weeks I was enjoying the colourful picture of my garden in bloom, but not for long.

Sadly the leaves disappeared from the marigolds, followed by the flowers, until there was nothing left but the stalks. Meanwhile both pansies and geraniums flourished.

Soon afterwards, my neighbour was gardening while I was sitting enjoying the autumn sun. We got chatting about our gardens and I happened to mention the fate of my marigolds.

"Oh, that'll be the snails," she said, adding that she had had hyacinths which had suffered the same fate. "Well, at least your marigolds and my hyacinths have made somebody happy!"

Suddenly, a glint of sunshine lit up a silvery zig-zagging of trails, catching my attention.

I wondered if these glistening snail trails traced a dance of celebration or even a thank-you note for their feast at my expense.

Perhaps I should find solace in the fact that her hyacinths had made somebody happy and apply the same maxim to my marigolds.

Gardens are full of lessons for living. Jesus, himself once mistaken for a gardener, spoke of planting seeds, growing plants and reaping a harvest as a vivid picture of his Kingdom.

"The Kingdom of God is like this. A man went out to sow . . ."

How thrilling it is to be partners in the miracle of growth in our gardens, where his parables still bloom whatever the season. ■

Believe In
Yourself

By Rev. Susan Sarapuk

LOVE Wimbledon. Over recent years a lot of younger players have started to come through, including twenty-year-old Canadian Eugenie Bouchard, who made it through to the finals in 2014.

When she was interviewed prior to the match she was asked if she was surprised to have come so far in the championship. She replied that no, she expected it of herself because she'd put in a lot of work over the years. She didn't sound at all conceited; it was a level-headed assessment of her current position.

It made me think about how we regard ourselves. How many of us are really satisfied with who and where we are? I suspect many of us suffer from an element of self-doubt, even in our relationship with God.

We are brought up to have insecurities – about our appearance, our achievements, whether we are likeable people. As we get older there are increasing pressures to stay looking young and not let ourselves go. Sometimes we are our own harshest critics; we never feel good enough.

That can often spill over into our thoughts about God. Surely we couldn't possibly be good enough for him? If we were a disappointment to our parents and to ourselves, then we must be a disappointment to God, too. But to think like that is to impose our thoughts and our standards on God and to refuse to accept what he tells us is our position.

"God so loved the world that he gave his only Son," John tells us in

iStock.

John 3:16.

Jesus didn't come to condemn the world. When he saw people he had compassion. Jesus chose flawed men to be his disciples. Who could be more flawed than Peter, who was full of bravado yet proved to be a coward at the moment of testing when he deserted Jesus? If anyone had cause to see themselves as a failure, Peter did, yet Jesus restored him and gave him a

commission to lead the church.

God believed in Peter. God believed in Paul, the great persecutor who smirked as he watched Stephen being stoned to death. God believes in us.

"See, I have engraved you on the palm of my hands; your walls are ever before me." (Isaiah 49:16.)

Jesus often said about the Pharisees that they made burdens for men's backs and did not help them to carry them. For them, religion was all about keeping a set of rules and working hard to be good enough. That's the kind of religion many of us still suffer from.

Jesus said he had come to bring life. He came to deal with sin so that we could know the love of God, to know that we are accepted. We are not the problem – sin is, and there is a solution:

"God made him who had no sin to be sin for us, so that in him we might become the righteousness of God." (2 Corinthians 5:21.)

So, just as Eugenie Bouchard was confident in her position in the tennis world, so we can be secure in our position in Christ. The work has been done. This is where we belong, in the love of God.

Ultimately it's a choice for all of us – to continue living in self-condemnation, or to accept that God really does love us with all our flaws and insecurities. And when we can accept that, then we are set free to be the joyous, welcoming ambassadors for the gospel he wants us to be. ■

Time To
Listen

By Janice Ross

AS a student in Edinburgh years ago, I was shown hospitality by members of the church which I attended. Often I shared meals of lovely Sunday roasts, served on spotless white tablecloths with Sunday-best plates and cutlery.

It was always such a great treat to be welcomed into a home and served a lovely home-made meal rather than to eat in the student refectory.

But one home was my favourite. Mrs McKinley, a widow, lived in a small flat. She made the most wonderful soup.

A meal with her consisted of a steaming bowl of home-made broth, a chunk of bread and a boiled egg.

It wasn't what I ate that made these Sundays so memorable; quite simply, it was the special company.

There was a warmth of welcome and peace in Mrs McKinley's home that made me long to be invited back. She was a very ordinary elderly lady but a good listener.

We would sit around the fire after our lunch and she would listen and I would chat.

Mrs McKinley taught me how to make flank of mutton soup and chicken broth, and I still serve up her recipes.

Years later, I met a lady coming out of church one day.

"I know you," she said. "You were a fourth-year student in Edinburgh when I was just in my first year. You invited me to your flat for a meal."

iStock.

I didn't remember her.

"I hope I gave you something tasty to eat," I said.

"Oh, yes, I always remember it," she answered. "You gave me spaghetti bolognese. I'd never heard of it before. I didn't know how to eat it. I had a new white blouse on and I slurped the sauce all down it!"

Oops! My hospitality had been memorable, but not in the way I would have liked. Unfortunately, I had made this young student feel uncomfortable.

Did I give her time to chat? Did I listen and care? These thoughts were uppermost in my mind. Perhaps I did, but at the end of the day that is not what she remembered.

Jesus was invited to a home once, that of two sisters, Mary and Martha.

The story goes that Martha busied herself making food and getting all hot and bothered, while Mary just sat and listened to her guest.

Poor Martha finally exploded in front of her visitor.

"Sit at my feet and listen"

"Lord, don't you care that my sister has left me to do all the work by myself?"

We may have expected Jesus to have taken Martha's side. After all, it's not fair that one person should have to do all the work and get so stressed, is it?

But Jesus didn't say that!

"Actually, Mary has chosen what is better. She has chosen to sit at my feet and listen."

Many people find that very unfair of Jesus.

After all, Martha was doing a good and kind thing in trying to feed all those guests.

But Jesus was not telling Martha off.

He loved her enough to say, "Slow down, dear Martha. Don't get distracted with things like food, which are very nice but not the most important thing right at this moment.

"Come and sit down and listen and just enjoy being with me."

So the next time we entertain, let's remember it's not about the food – it's about enjoying one another's company. ■

Breathe New *Life*

By Rev. Ian Petrie

A YEAR ago, a friend of mine gave me a fuchsia pot plant, accompanied by what has turned out to be a timely, not to say prophetic, warning.

"Ian," Bill said, well aware of my erratic and somewhat destructive gardening, "this should do well this year, but fuchsias are famously temperamental and it may struggle next year. Look after it."

Well, my fuchsia excelled itself last year, producing a lasting and ever-changing array of buds bursting into flower from spring right through to November. The leaves lasted even longer before succumbing to the winter chill.

That was last year, however. This year, January, February and March saw a steady decline – so much so that in mid-April, I had reluctantly pronounced my fuchsia dead.

"Abide in me and I will abide in you"

One evening I pulled it from its pot, the dead wood coming away in my hands, and I placed it on the grass ready for throwing out the next day.

Fortunately my daughter, Fiona, visited and saved the day – for my fuchsia, anyway.

She espied the empty pot first and then the displaced fuchsia, its erstwhile occupant, still clothed in its soil. Then, shaking her head, she

iStock.

pointed out some tiny green shoots, which I had dismissed as intrusive weeds.

How wrong I was!

I apologised to my fuchsia and immediately returned it to its home.

Through the next weeks, I checked it on a daily basis and, sure enough, the tiny shoots expanded to a few leaves before multiplying into many leaves.

At the time of writing this, those leaves are now dominating the plant and, dare I say it, there is a suggestion of other buds, which hopefully will blossom into beautiful and colourful fuchsia flowers.

"I am the true vine," Jesus once said, "and my Father is the husbandman. He breaks off every branch that does not bear fruit; he prunes every branch that bears fruit, so that it will be clean and bear more fruit."

Well, in my defence, what I was doing with my fuchsia was a kind of rough pruning, just part of my practice of coarse gardening! But then Jesus goes to the heart of the matter and growth in these powerful words.

"Abide in me, and I will abide in you; whoever abides in me, and I in him, will bear much fruit."

What I was forgetting in my rough pruning was the part of my fuchsia plant which was the hidden part, the source of all its growing power, namely the roots. Even uprooting it did not kill it! Ingeniously, the roots would reach out to access some other source of nourishment, ever working for the health of its plant.

I am reminded that Mary Magdalene once mistook her Risen Lord for a gardener. Perhaps unawares, she was recognising Jesus in a profoundly true guise, for he tends the very roots of our being to enable us to grow.

Growing is not a one-off event but an annual miracle of renewal, even rebirth, spanning both time and eternity. ■

The Language Of
Love

By Rev. Ian W.F. Hamilton

WHEN down in London my wife and I always pay a visit to the South Bank of the Thames. There are usually some wonderful concerts, exhibitions and events taking place at that venue.

We didn't have to look very long or hard to discover that, while we were there, a summer "Festival Of Love" was the Southbank Centre's highlight. In fact, a notice advertising it was emblazoned high above the centre, clearly visible from the other side of the famous river!

Welcome To Our Festival Of Love, the notice read, and so we duly accepted.

We soon discovered that this festival was taking place to explore and to celebrate human relationships in all their forms. We all have feelings for other people, but these feelings differ depending on the particular people and circumstances.

In the English language we only have one word to describe these feelings – namely, "love". However, this wasn't always the case. Greek is one of the richest of all languages and it has an unrivalled power to express the different shades of meaning.

The Ancient Greeks had around 30 words to describe love. There, at the Southbank's Festival of Love, some of the most powerful Greek words were chosen to help guide patrons towards a greater understanding of this emotion which makes the world go round!

Among the most powerful Greek "love" definitions we discovered "Storge", "Eros" and "Agape".

"Storge" is related to family affection, the kind of love parents have for children and children for parents. "Eros" normally refers to the love a man has for a woman, the physical love between the sexes, reminding us of the London landmark in the centre of Piccadilly Circus.

"Agape", however, is something quite different. This expression of love is the principle by which we should live. It's the love of humanity.

We can't help loving our families and dear ones – blood is thicker than water, as they say. We can't help falling in love, either. Although the experience is something very precious, this kind of love isn't an achievement, it's something that just happens!

"Storge" and "Eros" are connected with the heart. But "Agape" is connected with the mind, to live in such a way that we love one another despite everything, even our enemies.

That demands an attitude of will that conquers our natural emotions. "Agape" is Christian love, namely one which implores us to love those we don't like!

It doesn't ask us to love them in the same way we love our families and those closest to us, but it does implore us always to seek to help them.

That is why the Greeks had these different words to express this feeling of love.

At the Southbank Festival of Love you can visit the Temple of Agape, which celebrates the power of love to conquer hate.

This is the kind of love St Paul was thinking about when he wrote his immortal words, "The greatest of these is love."

Welcome To Our Festival Of Love. That's a sign that could be emblazoned outside every church up and down the land, because that is what Christianity is all about! ■

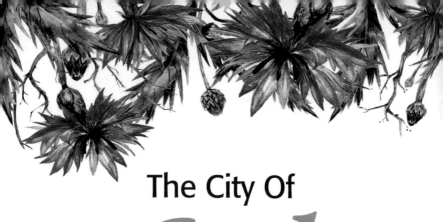

The City Of

God

By Rev. Andrew Watson

CHESTER is a university city in the north of England, close to the Welsh border. It's very popular with tourists, who love its picturesque mediaeval buildings.

Indeed, it has a long and colourful history, with records of a Roman fort there as early as the first century AD.

King Arthur and King Alfred also have associations with the area. One of its more recent claims to fame is as the birthplace of actor Daniel Craig, better known as Special Agent 007.

Chester is renowned for the almost perfectly preserved city walls which surround the old town area.

You can walk round them still, pausing to admire the city gates or old-style streets.

Romans, Saxons, Normans and James Bonds have all come and gone, but these steadfast walls remain.

One of the images of the age to come, given by Christ to his apostle John in the book of Revelation, chapters 21 and 22, is of a city – the "new" Jerusalem.

Some people may think of modern cities in terms of noise, overcrowding, pollution and traffic jams.

But this city is described in ideal terms – spacious, with firm foundations, strong walls and ever-open gates.

Safe and secure, with room for everyone!

iStock.

assures us there will be no more crying, sorrow or pain for God's people, for death itself has passed away.

As with almost every other page of Holy Scripture, the last page of the Bible combines these beautiful words of comfort and encouragement with a final challenge.

In no uncertain terms, it is made clear that there is no place in God's city for those who unashamedly practise immorality, idolatry, violence or fraud.

The welcome is for the humble – those who profess humble, penitent faith in Jesus.

"Blessed are those who wash their robes, that they may have the right to the tree of life and may go through the gates into the city." (John v 14.)

They will know everlasting, heavenly security.

Well has this hymn-writer put it:

Glorious things of thee are spoken,
Zion, city of our God;
He whose word cannot be broken
Formed thee for his own abode. ◼

It appears to be made from gold and precious gems. It is a garden city – the "river of the water of life" runs through its heart, watering the "tree of life" which provides leaves with healing properties for all nations.

It is a place of refuge and peace which is well supplied and outstandingly beautiful.

There will be no more evicted or homeless people. There will be no more poverty or threat. Nor will there be any sickness or disability in the city of God and Christ.

It will be a place of supreme wellbeing. No more sin or consequence thereof! Revelation

"Home, Sweet Home" and "Home is where the heart is". These two sayings speak volumes in a few words. Shakespeare wrote in "As You Like It": "When I was at home, I was in a better place." May your home be your better place – always.

Joining
The Dots

By Kathrine Davey, Mansfield Methodist preacher

SALOME is the name of the lady we've been investigating in our Bible study group recently.

She is mentioned by name in just one of the four gospels, yet there are so many traces of her in other places, as a wife, a mother and disciple. That is why I called her the dot-to-dot lady of the Gospels.

Salome was mentioned as one of the women who were there when Jesus was dying on the cross. She was also one of the women who came to anoint his body on the Sunday morning and who then became one of the first witnesses to the resurrection of Christ.

She was probably the mother of James and John, who were among the first disciples of Jesus, called to leave their fishing boats behind with their father, Zebedee.

Yet she did not grumble when she had to give up her sons who went out to be with Jesus. In fact, she became a follower of Jesus herself, and was described as one of a group of women "of means" who supported Jesus and looked after his practical needs during his time on earth.

This was probably financed by Zebedee's fishing business – after all, he is described as having hired men, so his business couldn't have been doing that badly. But he was prepared to give away his profits so that Jesus's business could prosper.

I doubt that Salome realised that she would be called upon to pay

the ultimate sacrifice – the death of her son. Like the disciples, she knew that Jesus's ministry was a dangerous one, yet she supported both her sons in this precarious venture.

And her fears were not unfounded. James was martyred by Herod for his faith; he is described as the first disciple to be killed. Her other son, John, was the disciple beloved by Jesus, the one who would take Mary into his home after Jesus had died. Perhaps he is even the writer of the Gospel of John, who died in exile.

It is often the same in our everyday lives. People we think we know well leave little clues to a part of their lives that we never knew existed. Unfortunately this is often too late to find out the little details that were missing from our knowledge of someone.

I have often been surprised when it is only in a funeral memorial service that I begin to really appreciate what that person has done. And by then it is too late.

But it still gives me the opportunity to "join the dots" and find out some information that was missing in my knowledge of that person.

Many people are also what might be seen as "hidden" witnesses to Jesus. Not in the sense, I hope, that they hide away their commitment and love for him, but rather in the sense that they, too, will probably not find their names presented boldly in some holy book about their witness.

> **"Many great jewels have their worth underestimated"**

So, when their life is over, someone will have to "connect the dots" to see how Jesus formed and changed their lives, and how they played their parts in being part of his.

Many great jewels have their worth underestimated until a sale or auction reveals their true value, and some insignificant object may turn out to possess great worth because of their association with someone important.

Just little glimpses here and there can reveal a whole story just waiting to be told. ■

Follow The
Light

By Rev. Ian W.F. Hamilton

RECENTLY we took a trip down memory lane when we flew from Dundee airport to visit Jersey in the Channel Islands. It was several years since we were last there with our family when they were still young, so we decided to revisit the venues we had all enjoyed.

Our first port of call was the magnificent Corbière Lighthouse, erected to warn shipping of the rugged coastline around the island.

Standing high on the island's south-west coast, it can be seen from 18 miles away, and it's one of Jersey's most photographed buildings. Fortunately, the tide was out, enabling us to walk out over the long causeway to get really close to it.

Lighthouses nowadays are in the main fully automated, especially those situated on remote coastlines and islands. Their powerful beams are often controlled by computers hundreds of miles away.

Corbière Lighthouse on Jersey was automated back in 1976. Most of us can well remember the faithful service given by those who manned our lighthouses around our coast.

These good folks were often cut off from their homes and families for the period of a tour of duty lasting several months, a sacrifice which was necessary in order that the ships of the sea journeyed safely across the waters.

Corbière reminded me of a story I once told the children in church. It

iStock.

concerned an old man who had been a lighthouse keeper.

One wet and windy night, so the story goes, the man took out of his drawer a taper.

He lit it and, just before he began to climb up the long, winding staircase inside his lighthouse, his small grandson, who was visiting, frowned.

"Where are you taking that light, Grandad?"

"Away up high, in fact, right up to the very top of the lighthouse," Grandad replied.

"And what are you going to do with it when you get there?" the little boy asked.

"I'm going to use it to show the ships out at sea where the harbour is. It's very stormy out there in the North Sea tonight and at this very minute there could well be some ships looking desperately for a light to help guide them into the harbour."

"But no ship could ever see that light – it's far too small!"

"Follow me up to the top and leave the rest to me," the old man replied.

When he reached the top of the lighthouse, with the small taper he lit the great lamps with their brightly polished reflectors which stood behind them.

The result was that a terrific blaze of light was shed for miles around for all the ships to see, and to help guide them safely home to their harbour. The light from the taper was small, but it was used to do great things.

This, of course, was the lesson I drew from the story I was telling to the children in church. It is a lesson every one of us would do well to learn, namely that we must never think of our service, our contribution, our light as being too small.

We must keep our light burning, keep offering our gifts and our service to God and leave the rest to him, because he can do marvellous things with whatever we offer. ■

Come Safely

Home

By Rev. Andrew Watson

WE moved to North Donegal in the wintry month of January. The first few days were freezing, dark and incredibly stormy. Between the front door and the car everybody was having a bad hair day!

Once the storm subsided we got out to explore and discovered we had neighbours – the guys in the picture on the right, who look remarkably like the cast of the TV animation "Shaun The Sheep". They live in the field next door to us.

When I come out of my door they raise their heads and look at me quizzically as if to say, "Yes?" They even come over to the fence to see if I have anything for them.

There are 10 of them, easily countable for they seem to be fairly comfortable sharing space, and follow each other up and down the field constantly. They even have a little rocky hillock on which they congregate to study the view over the appropriately named Sheephaven Bay.

It makes me wonder what happened to the one that got lost in Jesus's parable (Luke 15: 4-7). If sheep are so inclined to follow each other, even if it's through a hole in the fence into harm's way, what happened to this one? How did he get separated from the others? Did he just get tired and fall behind, or was he distracted by some juicy-looking grass to the left or right of the path?

Did he then feel a little guilty and embarrassed about rejoining his pals, or maybe get stuck in a boggy

iStock.

patch? Easy enough if you're thirsty and seeking water.

I'm told that a sheep that gets stranded in a bog is helpless to save itself and panics. When it is pulled out it is literally shaking and unable to walk. That adds authenticity to Jesus's description of the shepherd having to hoist the poor beast on to his shoulders to bring it safely home to the sheep pen.

I'm looking at these fellas next door and I don't fancy trying to lift one, never mind carting it any distance. Fair play to those who sometimes do!

And thanks and praise to the Good Shepherd Jesus, who doesn't abandon us when we fall behind, but comes looking for us, and who carried our sin and shame on the cross at Calvary that we might be brought safe home to the haven God has prepared!

He isn't content with 99 when there is meant to be 100. He grieves for the one who is still out there, wandering and in danger. He "came to seek and to save that which was lost."(Luke 19: 10). He is eager to forgive those who want to be rescued.

We are told he knows and calls each of his sheep by name. He has gone ahead of us, even through suffering and death, so that we may trustingly follow and not be overcome by fear, for we are on the way home.

And home with the Good Shepherd is a good place to be. ■

Selective
Hearing

By Kathrine Davey, Mansfield Methodist preacher

WHEN my own children were small or if we had small people come to visit, I noticed that whenever we told them to do anything that they didn't want to do, they put their hands over their ears and sang loudly to shut out the sound. It was as though they were saying, "I can't hear you."

I am sure that this is a situation most people are familiar with, whether it is when we are dealing with our own children or grandchildren. I have noticed that they claim not to be able to hear when I ask each one to tidy his room, yet they suddenly are able to hear perfectly when I announce that dinner's ready!

This "selective hearing" continues throughout our lives, but we learn not to be so obvious about it. Because it is often very true that we only hear the things that we choose.

Yet, on the other hand, we expect God to be on 24-hour "listening duty"!

As the Psalmist says, "Evening, morning and noon I cry out in distress", but then he adds, "and he hears my voice". If God listens to us, we should listen to him.

It never fails to amaze me, when I am preparing a Sunday service, how the same portion of God's word can result in such a completely different sermon when delivered by another preacher. This is because God treats us all as individuals who need to hear different things on every single occasion.

iStock.

Jesus told a story about those who hear God's word, and there are several different ways of reacting to it. It is often called the parable of the sower. The same batch of seed was scattered and fell on to different kinds of ground. Three out of the four – that is, the vast majority – fell on bad ground.

They fell on the path to be eaten by the birds, on rocky soil or surrounded by weeds. Only one quarter of the possibilities was well received and grew strongly.

This is one of the few parables that is explained by Jesus, as he obviously thought it was an important lesson to learn. That blank look, or outright hostility, which is often directed at us when we bring Christ or Christian views into the conversation, may rather be a reflection on our message.

All the parables illustrate the Lord's way of finding a method of linking what he has to say to the things in which his listeners were interested – homes, families, coins, farms, vines, wheat, weeds, seed, food, pearls, buildings as well as many others.

"If God listens to us, we should listen to him"

He tells us not to worry, not by using long, academic words but by talking about birds and flowers! He describes his followers in terms of salt and light. It is not surprising that those people who were most opposed to him had spent years in study.

Yet Jesus did not spend hours in philosophical debate, as he was more concerned with relating to the ordinary people. In fact, there are several mentions throughout the gospels of the crowds that thronged to hear Jesus.

These same crowds forced him to seek solitude on various occasions. It was at such moments that he sought time alone to be with God, "tuning out" the worries of the world that he had left behind him.

The selective hearing that Jesus displayed at these moments enabled him to focus on God. In fact, the Bible says many times that he spent many hours, even whole evenings and on at least one occasion a whole night, in prayer to his father. So perhaps there is a lesson to be learned from the children, after all! ■

A Happier
Place

By Maggie Ingall

A **FEW** days ago I bumped into a friend of mine who had just collected her young grandson from school.

"I'm six now," he informed me proudly. "It was my birthday last week, and I had a party with sausage rolls and cakes, and I got given this!"

He delved into his coat pocket and, with a flourish, brought out a small multicoloured patchwork mouse.

"It was his favourite present," Sally explained with a smile. "It's funny how, out of all the bigger and more expensive gifts he received, it was that little mouse that has been most appreciated."

I had to smile with her, for it's a phenomenon that I have frequently noticed myself. It is indeed so often the smallest things in life, whether gifts, words or deeds, that are valued the most.

In some cases they might even be so small that the giver themselves can't even remember them!

I had first-hand experience of this when I went to a school reunion – and no, I will not reveal just how many years had passed since I left! It was wonderful to catch up with old friends once more, exchange news and reminisce about days long gone by.

There were even some of our former teachers present. One of them I was especially glad to see again, for she had been my tutor at a time when I had been particularly anxious about my

iStock.

102

studies, wondering about what to do with my life and if I would ever be good at anything.

The advice and encouragement which she had given me only took a couple of minutes of her time, but the effect on me has turned out to be both beneficial and long lasting.

"Mrs Squires!" I greeted her with some enthusiasm and reminded her of the incident. "You'll never know how much your words meant to me."

"I'm so glad." She smiled back. "But, though I remember you very well, I can't recall what I said. Nothing very momentous, I suspect, but I'm very pleased that it helped."

It had! Something similar happened when I met an old neighbour.

"We often think of you," he told me one day. "We remember how you saved our family holiday."

"What?" I enquired, baffled.

"You looked after our dog for a fortnight when the kennels let us down just before we were to leave for the airport," he reminded me. "I thought we would have to cancel the trip, then you stepped into the breach and offered to look after her for the fortnight."

I was pleased that he remembered me so kindly, but until he mentioned the incident I could have barely recalled it!

So, what am I trying to say? Simply that Sally's story about the little patchwork mouse reinforced my belief that little things really do mean a lot.

Not one of us needs to be a giant, a leader or a slayer of dragons in order to make a difference to the planet. It only needs a kind deed, a word of encouragement, a gesture of thoughtfulness to make the world the happier place that we'd all like it to be.

Better still, the opportunity for doing such things is far more likely than the chances of coming across a rogue dragon.

At least – I hope it is! ■

Stay
Passionate

By Rev. Susan Sarapuk

WHAT are you passionate about in life? One of the things that brings me great joy is playing tennis. I play once a week at the local tennis centre with a group of middle-aged women.

I love to hit the ball hard; I love to run. Sometimes, if we're an odd number, one of the young men employed at the tennis centre will give me a game, and nothing is better than being challenged by someone who's younger and better than you. Who cares about the creaking knees and aching limbs afterwards?

I love to follow tennis, too. I've been to Wimbledon a number of times and every summer I'm glued to the television while the tournament's on. If I had subscription TV I'd probably spend most of my time watching tennis,

so it's a good thing I don't!

Back in the Nineties I was passionate about "Star Trek – The Next Generation". My friend and I bought all the videos and magazines and over a period of three years we attended a number of conventions.

People dressed up in costume, there were sales rooms where you could buy anything related to "Star Trek" and there were regular screenings of episodes and talks by cast members. (I was once in a lift with George Takei – Sulu.)

John was passionate about Jesus. In his first letter he writes, "That which was from the beginning, which we have heard, which we have seen with our eyes, which we have looked at and our hands have touched – this we proclaim."

You can sense the excitement behind those words.

iStock.

"Listen, I've seen him! I know this is true!"

He had a passion to communicate it, as did all the believers who saw the Risen Jesus. How could they not, after everything they'd been through?

There's a passion, too, in Thomas, who wasn't present the first time Jesus appeared in the upper room.

"Unless I see the nail marks in his hands and put my finger where the nails were and put my hand into his side I will not believe it." (John 20:25.)

We often deride Thomas for doubting, but I sense passion behind those words.

"I really want to see him!" Thomas is saying. And as soon as he gets his wish he proclaims, "My Lord and my God!"

Could anyone be more passionate than the apostle Paul, who counted his old life as rubbish compared to knowing Jesus as Lord?

So, what about me? Am I still passionate about the Risen Lord, or have I become jaded over the years?

It's easy for that to happen when the good news is no longer fresh, when we've got used to the message of the Gospel. We forget what a privilege it is to be a Christian and to have the assurance of God's forgiveness and love.

Maybe that was the problem of the church in Laodicea, which is accused of being lukewarm in the book of Revelation. Speaking as a member of the Anglican church, I think we can turn being lukewarm into a fine art! We don't want to bother anyone or intrude into their lives.

That certainly wasn't the attitude of the first Christians. They'd seen something that was life-changing for the whole world and they needed to tell others.

God still wants disciples who are passionate about the resurrection. If I can be passionate about tennis and "Star Trek", which are really unimportant in the grand scheme of things, surely I should be passionate about the Lord who died and rose again for me? ■

Watch
Over Me

By Kathrine Davey, Mansfield Methodist preacher

A FEW days ago, I was on a course where we went to see the CCTV control room where the cameras that are continually watching our town have their images displayed on rows and rows of computer screens.

We were all impressed with how detailed and focused the cameras were, and how clear the pictures that came from them proved to be.

In most cases, the cameras are not static, but slowly pan around to take in a very wide panorama of shops, banks, cafés etc., and I was shown how they can zoom in or out at the computer operator's whim.

Then, as a person moves out of range of one town centre camera, he or she is picked up by another.

This continues throughout, whether we are dashing about between shops or relaxing on a night out with friends.

Although some people might find it a bit of a threat, I find it quite comforting to know that God is all around us, continually caring for us, and protecting us from harm.

Many a crime has been prevented by these cameras and, in the same way, we do not know how many harmful things God's protection has saved us from. In the Old Testament, Hagar, who was the servant of Sarah, Abraham's wife, talks of "the God who sees me".

Although there were no cameras around, God was able to "zoom in" on the runaway, and ensure she was treated in a kindly manner.

We are constantly reminded

iStock.

throughout the Bible that God is all-seeing and all-knowing. The psalmist asks himself, "Where can I go from your Spirit? Where can I flee from your presence?" This thought has given comfort to many throughout the centuries.

The song "From A Distance" has been recorded by many artists and, while it speaks of the wonders of God's creation, it does not tell the whole story – God is not distant, but is tirelessly watching over each one of us, surrounding us with his care.

I was able to be there that morning because most of us there, me included, go out as volunteers in groups every Saturday evening, to mix with and help those people, mainly young people, who are out on the town to make the most of their weekend.

Groups of these people, usually from local churches, do the same all over the county on Saturday evenings until the early hours of Sunday morning.

We have quite a few conversations with those we meet, and many are surprised that we are all there representing churches, as the common view is that God is only present in a building and is only able to greet visitors on Sunday mornings.

We agree with them that God is present on Sundays, but he is also there on the other six days of the week. In fact, this view is echoed by Brother Lawrence, a 17th-century monk, whose book "The Practice Of The Presence Of God" says God can be with us anywhere – even when doing the washing-up!

His rule of spirituality and prayer was developed while involved in the tedious chores of cooking and cleaning at the beck and call of others.

He points out that as we come to realise that Christ is working in our lives, gradually a new image emerges. This image of us reflects that of the town-centre cameras which are there for our protection. ■

Write down all the good things you have in your life. This will very probably help you to have a good night's sleep and subconsciously set you up for a good day tomorrow. We should all count our blessings, and think positively.

Where The
Heart Is

By Rev. Susan Sarapuk

MY elderly father died recently and I've been clearing out the house I grew up in. It's amazing how much stuff is accumulated over a lifetime!

Not that my parents cluttered up the house by having loads of things on display, but when new items were bought the old ones got shunted into cupboards instead of being thrown away. I've found things I thought were lost in the mists of time.

Because I live in a small bungalow and can't accommodate anything extra, all the furniture and most of the knick-knacks they built up over the years will have to go to charity or to landfill. It has taught me that it's good to have a clear-out from time to time.

Clearing my parents' house has made me spring-clean my own. I was already hoarding videos I could never play again, simply because it was easier to shove them in a cupboard than to take them to the local recycling site.

When we're young and trying to define who we are in the world, possessions seem more important. They tell people about our tastes and where to place us in the scheme of things.

We're still permitted to like nice things when we're older – after all, we want our homes to be welcoming. But they shouldn't be the focus of our lives.

Jesus said, "A man's life does not consist in the abundance of his possessions." Jesus's disciples left everything to follow him; families

iStock.

and thriving businesses in some cases.

Jesus warned us that becoming a disciple could be tough. He said not to store up treasures on earth where moths and rust destroy and thieves break in and steal.

He told the parable of the rich man who gathered everything into barns and, well-satisfied with his provision for the future, thought he could just sit back and relax, not realising that he was going to die that night. There was the rich young man who tried to keep the law but couldn't respond to Jesus's invitation to sell what he had and follow him.

Wealth and possessions got in the way of what was meaningful.

What about clearing out our spiritual lives?

There is an opportunity to do this every time we gather for a service, as we say the prayer of confession together. But we don't have to wait for Sunday, we can begin every day with a clean slate with God.

So the things that weigh us down we can let go of. After all, if we're disciples we should be travelling light!

I suppose we hold on to stuff because it's full of memories. I've found looking at old photos particularly poignant.

Although I'll never see the house in reality as it was, I can still see it captured on film along with my younger, healthier parents. I've discovered that a house is just a house without the people you love inhabiting it, so getting rid of their possessions hasn't been as hard as I thought it would be.

What I will remember about my parents is the love and security they provided when I was growing up; the fact that they stayed together even when the going got tough. They might not have had the latest TV or sofa, but I felt blessed.

Things mean very little in the end. I wonder, when it's our time to go, whether we will be remembered for our beautiful homes and the lovely things we possessed, or for the sort of people we were. ∎

> ## "Things mean very little in the end"

Give
Thanks

By Rev. Andrew Watson

MY wife and I had slipped out for a walk, as we often do. It was dark and the footpaths were slippery with wet leaves. There was no wind that night and the air was mild for November, but still our mood was sombre.

Some issues were weighing heavily; problems and strained relationships had lately been taking their toll.

As we walked the deserted streets, hand in hand, we felt as though we hadn't a friend in the world.

In the midst of the gloom the lights were still on in one of our local chip shops, though the blinds were drawn, and through the door we could see a young lad mopping the floor.

We got a rare urge for a chip, and when we pushed the door it was still open. Inside, it was warm, and the woman behind the high counter was smiling and chatting to the last few customers of the evening.

We didn't wait until we got home, but shared our chips from the paper bag as we walked and talked. My wife had said she only wanted one or two, but ended up taking quite a few!

They were fresh, salty and delicious – easily the nicest chips we've had in years. We finished them to the very last one, just as we turned in at the manse gate.

That night, while our hearts remained anxious and the future uncertain about some things, we gave thanks.

iStock.

Thanks for the chips, and the couple of coins I'd found left in my pocket to get them, and for the light and the lady with her friendly smile. Thanks for each other, still together and close after all these years, and for our family.

Thanks for a measure of health and strength and freedom to be able to walk around a few blocks, and go about our business each day. Thanks that the sun will rise again tomorrow, a new day, with new opportunities.

Thanks to the Lord, who understands and so willingly forgives us; whose love never fails. Thanks that he is working out his purpose despite our many human weaknesses and failings.

There is a plan, and somehow it will all be OK, even if it hurts in the short term.

The Apostle Paul, in one of his most personal and heartfelt letters in the New Testament, writes: "We are hard-pressed on every side, but not crushed; perplexed, but not in despair; persecuted, but not abandoned; struck down, but not destroyed." (2 Corinthians 4 v8,9.)

He feels fragile, like a jar made of humble clay; nevertheless, he's aware that inside he has real treasure, for God has shone into his heart "the light of the knowledge of the glory of God in the face of Christ" (v6).

The night may close in around us, but Christians are comforted by the constant presence of our faithful Saviour friend. Even though we may have to suffer a "thorn in the flesh" for a time, he promises his grace will be "sufficient" for us.

Therefore we are persuaded to do as the Bible instructs and give thanks "in all circumstances", for God is with us and he is powerful and gracious to provide our every need, even down to a poke of chips and a friendly smile on a dark evening! ■

Beyond
Words

by Rev. Ian Petrie

GRAEME, our eldest son, is forty-five and severely autistic. When he was seven, it became apparent that it was no longer in anyone's best interest for him to be cared for at home, and there began his journey through many different institutions.

Despite excellent care in all these places, Graeme, in these alien environments, regressed to the point where he gave no sign of knowing us, not even allowing us the eye contact which we had striven to achieve in his earlier years.

The first chink of light happened in Strathmartine Hospital in Dundee, with the building of three customised flats within its grounds. For the first time since leaving the family home over 20 years previously, Graeme had a room of his own, on his own.

He shared the flat with seven others, all more like himself, enjoying the peace and quiet of their own company, with one exception!

After a cautious start, Graeme began to thrive. Visiting Graeme became a pleasure as, for the very first time, we knew that he recognised us.

His carers were, by and large, the same as in Strathmartine. They knew Graeme and their affectionate care led him to blossom in this more benign environment.

Sitting in his room, decorated by his assigned carer, Mark, to suit his needs and style, we thought

iStock.

Graeme was happier than he had ever been. But the best was still to come, as word filtered through that Graeme was going to go into the community. This was pioneering for someone as vulnerable as Graeme, whose needs are 24/7 care.

My worries that he would not cope were allayed by Mark, who asked me if Graeme had progressed since coming into his flat. That was easy to answer!

"Well, then," Mark reassured me, "Graeme will flourish at least as much again with his own house and space."

And flourish Graeme most certainly has. After seven years he is flourishing still.

On my first visit, I was shown round his spacious house with its bright sitting-room, two bedrooms, kitchen and bathroom. I would have bought it myself on the spot!

"Why does Graeme need two bedrooms?" I asked.

"Why not?" his carer shot back. "Graeme is a thirty-eight-year-old man."

"It is always worthwhile to persevere"

And that is the secret of their wonderful care. They tend the needs not of an autistic adult, but of the person and personality of a thirty-eight-year-old man.

He has a car; he can't drive, and so has a chauffeur, with whom he goes to many different places. Just a few weeks ago, Graeme was brought to Edinburgh to visit me in my new home. He came in and looked around, found himself a comfortable seat and smiled.

All of a sudden he rose and went to explore my flat, which didn't take long, as there are only two rooms. He ate lunch and sat back, and I was aware of his gaze.

We looked at each other with an eloquence way beyond words. It seemed like after all these years I was looking past his condition and connecting with the real man beneath.

Relationships are seldom easy, whether we are interacting with family members, colleagues or strangers in the street. But in my experience it is always worthwhile to persevere. ■

A Free
Pass

By Rev. David Bryant

IT was 1956 and I had just finished the first year of my National Service as a private, serving at a training barracks in Aldershot. One of the perks of the job was that I was entitled to three free travel warrants a year to any destination in the British Isles.

I marched along to the Army Chaplain's office and asked if I could borrow a map book from him. I had decided to take full advantage of my first warrant and travel as far as possible!

My finger halted on Mallaig in northern Scotland. I did a bit of research and discovered that there was a night sleeper service I could take from King's Cross all the way there.

The company sergeant major stamped my travel warrant and then off I went. The sleeping car attendant showed me my berth. I was in luck for the other three beds were unoccupied.

I tucked into some sandwiches I had bought from the station buffet, had a cup of tea, and decided to turn in. It was the start of one of the most memorable journeys of my life, for I had not visited Scotland before.

The train pulled out of King's Cross with a whistle and a puff of steam. Then I must have dozed off, for I awoke to hear a voice in the small hours calling out "Edinburgh!" and then some time later a shout of "Glasgow!"

Some while later I pulled up the blind on the window and gasped in amazement. The train was slowly chugging through the most spectacular scenery I had ever seen. I slipped along to the dining

car and splashed out on a fried breakfast.

Then followed a wonderfully musical list of halts called out by the various station masters in rich Scottish accents – Tarbet, Ardlui, Crianlarich, Tyndrum, Bridge of Orchy.

At one station a pile of milk churns was loaded. At another, a shepherd in a long brown smock, carrying a crook, boarded with his dog. Just after Rannoch came a piece of high drama.

I pulled the leather strap to open the window for a breath of fresh, peat-filled air, but smelled burning. I looked down and, to my horror, I saw that one of the wheels on the next carriage was red hot.

Running along to the parcel van, I told the guard. He pulled the communication cord and we screeched to a stop.

Half an hour later a platelayer came along with a sledgehammer and knocked the jammed brake shoe free.

At long last, around about noon, we drew into Mallaig station.

I often think of life as being a journey; not on the night sleeper to Mallaig, but one on which we are looking out all the time for glimpses of God. There are so many places to find him!

We may see him in the beauty of Highland scenery, or a kindness shown us by a stranger. He may be present in the smile of a grandchild, or the happy faces of a couple being married.

I have come across our Lord, too, in the quiet courage of somebody who is ill. At birth we are given a free travel warrant for our journey through life. What a blessing and great gift it is. ■

For Your
Tomorrow

By Rev. Ian W.F. Hamilton

THE occasion of Remembrance is one that evokes memories of loved ones who were lost or wounded, or are still being lost and wounded in wars in our world.

In recent times, when we commemorated the centenary of the outbreak of WWI, the futility and global impact of war was hammered home to us as never before.

The Imperial War Museum in London was closed in 2014 in order to transform it to mark the WWI Centenary, creating ground-breaking galleries and a newly configured atrium to display the large iconic objects they have there relating to the Great War.

The Imperial War Museum in Manchester also staged wonderful events and exhibitions and told true stories of how war shapes lives, from a soldier's last letter home to the twisted steel from New York's former World Trade Center.

WWI ended in November 1918 when an armistice was declared so that peace terms could be arranged. At 11 a.m. on November 11, the last shot of the war was fired and for many years thereafter Armistice Day was observed on November 11. Now it is known as Remembrance Sunday and is always held on the second Sunday in November.

At the heart of Remembrance is the red poppy, used since 1920 to remember soldiers and service personnel who have died in wars. It was inspired by the WWI poem "In Flanders Fields" by Colonel John McCrae. McCrae described the Flanders poppy as the "Flower of Remembrance", and begins his poem thus:

In Flanders fields the poppies blow
Between the crosses, row on row,

iStock.

That mark our place; and in the sky
The larks, still bravely singing, fly
Scarce heard amid the guns below.

Poppies were first used by the American Legion to commemorate American soldiers lost in WW1, then they were adopted by military veterans' groups in Britain, Canada, Australia and New Zealand. Today, poppies commemorate servicemen and women who have been killed in all conflicts since.

The first Poppy Day was held in Britain on November 11, 1921. Field Marshal Earl Haig, who had been Commander-in-Chief in France, became the Founder-President of the newly formed British Legion. The Legion's purpose was then, as now, in times of need to bring aid to all men and women who have served in our Armed Forces, and to their widows and dependants.

In the early years after WWI, poppies were only worn on Remembrance Day itself, but now, thanks to the Royal British Legion's Poppy Appeal, poppies are widespread from October onwards and are worn by the public, politicians, members of the Royal Family and countless others. It has also become common to see poppies on cars, lorries, buses and trams. It is notable that the annual Poppy Appeal has a higher profile than any other charity in the UK.

At the heart of Remembrance, then, is the blood-red poppy, a symbol that reminds us of the millions who died in two mass slaughters, and in so many other wars in the world since, and as a result of acts of terrorism.

For ever, on this occasion, we will think of those who "gave their today for our tomorrow" and will give thanks for the sacrifice they made.

When we think of the blood-red poppy, we cannot but contemplate the blood that flowed from the Cross of Calvary and the supreme sacrifice made for us by the One who hung and suffered there. The One who gave up his life, a ransom for many, and the One who hauntingly said, "Remember me." ■

God's
Plan

By Rev. Susan Sarapuk

HOW many times have you heard the statement that there cannot be a God because of all the suffering in the world? It implies that either God doesn't care or that he isn't all-powerful, and who would want a God like that?

We constantly hear of earthquakes and famine in the news, of wars and terrorism, of accidents and people dying before their time. It doesn't seem fair. Why?

When someone poses a question like that it puts us on the spot. Often we don't know quite how to answer and sometimes it makes us question, too.

How can there be a God when there is so much suffering in the world?

My answer to the question is,

"How can there not be?"

If there is no God, then life really is random and cruel. Some people live to a good old age and others die still young; some people's lives are cruelly taken from them by others; some suffer indescribably.

Death wipes us out and that's it – tough luck if you got a bad draw. There is no recompense for evil, no justice, no sense that one day everything will be made right and we will understand. No, it's all random, and there seems no sense or purpose to life or death.

Christians have a promise of more on several levels.

"Do not let your hearts be troubled. Trust in God, trust also in me. In my Father's house are many rooms; if it were not so I would have told you. I am going

iStock.

there to prepare a place for you. And if I go and prepare a place for you I will come back and take you to be with me that you also may be where I am."

A friend of mine was a parish priest. The daughter of one of his parishioners had died in a fire on the other side of the world. The mother was continually haunted by images of the last moments of her child, imagining the fear and pain.

"Jesus would have come for her before that moment and taken her," my friend said.

There is the promise of more on the wider level of creation. We are told that the whole of creation has fallen, but it is God's plan to bring it back to wholeness.

"The creation itself will be liberated from its bondage to decay and brought into the glorious freedom of the children of God." (Romans 8:21.)

This is not the way the world was meant to be; it has been marred by sin. One day, Isaiah promises, "The wolf will live with the lamb and the leopard will lie down with the goat." (Isaiah 11:6.)

There is an acknowledgement that life can be tough; even when we're blessed in comparison to others, there are still struggles. But there will be a time when this is not so.

"He will wipe away every tear from their eyes. There will be no more death or mourning or crying or pain, for the old order of things has passed away." (Revelation 21:4.)

If there is no God then none of these things is true. If there is no God then life is random and cruel.

If there is a God then everything has meaning and purpose.

I know which option I prefer! ■

Winning The

Prize

By Rev. Ian Petrie

WHICH page of your newspaper do you turn to first? Amazingly, several would swoop in for a glance at the horoscopes, though few would admit to checking the stars!

Still more would open up the hatches, matches and despatches, painfully aware that the last-mentioned occupies by far the largest area, and checking that your own name isn't on the list!

Some would home in on the daily cartoon, hoping for a smile, while others stick with the headlines offering, more often than not, bad and disturbing news.

I do none of the above, joining the majority, at least of the male readership, in bouncing to the back of the paper – the sports pages.

There, in the sport of your choice, you can browse the ups and downs of the stars, whether they are winning or losing and, too often, whether they are injured or not. Did you know that the New Testament, as well as featuring the Wise Men following their star, also contains its very own sports pages and reports?

The Apostle Paul is the New Testament's chief sports correspondent, having once been a sportsman himself who had been forced to retire prematurely through injury. Paul saw his role as apostle to be versatile, being an agony uncle to many of the early Church's teething problems, using in the process these sporting metaphors.

"Surely you know that many runners take part in a race, but only

one of them wins the prize. Run, then, in such a way as to win the prize." Warming to his subject, Paul analyses the heart of the matter.

"Every athlete in training submits to strict discipline, in order to be crowned with a wreath that does not last; but we do it for one that will last for ever. That is why I run straight for the finishing line; that is why I'm like a boxer, who does not waste his punches. I harden my body with blows and bring it under complete control."

He turns his concentration to winning, emphasising that he keeps striving to win the prize.

"The one thing I do is to forget what is behind me and do my best to reach what is ahead. So I run straight for the finishing line towards the goal in order to win the prize."

One thing always niggled me about this scenario. As Paul himself admits, only one person can win the prize. What about the others in the race who arrive at the finishing line when the tape is already broken?

Paul answers that question when he defines the prize as that which Christ Jesus has already won. The site of that victory was Calvary, but the race had already been won in the stadium in the Garden of Gethsemane on the eve of his crucifixion, a victory which he shares with us, so that we can all feel the thrill of breaking that finishing tape as victors.

This is the race against self, raging within us all, and Paul suggests that if we don't live the struggle, we are already in danger of defeat.

Paul recounts sporting parables challenging us to faith in action, an active faith, involving hours of training and practice when we'd rather stay tucked up in bed. While demanding nothing less than his personal best, he challenges us to do likewise.

What would be read in the sports pages of our discipleship? ■

There is an old Russian proverb that says, "Every day is a messenger of God." A simple enough saying. Imagine if we took it seriously and began each day by listening to that message, then ended each day with our reply.

Published in Great Britain by D.C. Thomson & Co., Ltd.,
185 Fleet Street,
London EC4A 2HS